The Novels of

Hugh MacLennan

by ROBERT H. COCKBURN

ROBERT COCKBURN

Robert Cockburn was born in Portchester, N.Y. He studied at Colby College and the University of New Brunswick. His poems and reviews have appeared in publications in Canada, Ireland, and the U.S.A. The poetry has also been broadcast nationwide on the C.B.C. ("Anthology", "Gerussi"), while a chapbook of his verse, *Friday Night, Fredericton,* was published in 1968. Cockburn first worked in the English Department at Acadia University and has been teaching Canadian Literature at the University of New Brunswick since September 1967. He is a poetry editor of *The Fiddlehead.*

HUGH MACLENNAN

Copyright © Canada 1969 by Harvest House Ltd.
All rights reserved.
Library of Congress Catalog Card No. 76-109579.
ISBN-0-88772-108-7 (Paper)
ISBN-0-88772-109-5 (Cloth)
First printing March 1970.

For information address Harvest House Ltd.,
1364 Greene Avenue, Montreal 215, Quebec, Canada.
Printed and bound in Canada.

～ FOREWORD

CRITICISM of Canadian literature has always been an active front in the battle of the Canadian identity. The nationalists advance under the banner of Charles Heavysege; the cosmopolitans snipe at Bliss Carman, regroup and charge at Morley Callaghan. The Maple Leaf faction sends up balloons for Haliburton; the literary World Federalists cheerfully explode them. And no part of the terrain has seen more action than the fiction of Hugh MacLennan, the most overtly Canadian of all our novelists.

In a sense the argument finally turns on the stature of Canadian events, and the extent to which we feel they matter, or ought to matter, to anyone else. To some of us MacLennan has mattered very much, because he has tried to express our sense of a country we love, a country which we feel could well become, as one of MacLennan's characters puts it, priceless to mankind. For others, it is faintly dishonest not to say that anyone with a mature interest in fiction must distinguish between aesthetic satisfaction and a romantic vision of the Canadian possibility; criticism must address itself unsentimentally to the question of literary judgment, using the most rigorous and metropolitan standards. To love a demonstrably minor writer like Matthew Prior is one thing; to regard him as a major poet just because we love him is something else altogether.

In this study Robert Cockburn is firmly on the side of the cosmopolitans, and his praise, where he gives it, carries considerable weight because of the candour with which he discusses MacLennan's failings. Cockburn applies the accepted criteria for fiction and finds MacLennan distinctly deficient. The novels reveal a "poverty of imagination" and are seen to be ruinously didactic. MacLennan's characters are subordinate to theme and his themes are on the whole contrived and rather pompous. Cockburn is a poet, and he has a poet's pleasure in playing games with metaphor, occasionally to devastating effect: many critics have called characters "puppets" but Cockburn is capable of revitalizing the metaphor by adding that the puppets are wired for sound. It is a pleasure to run across so *readable* a literary study.

What I have said suggests that Cockburn is unsympathetic to MacLennan, which is not really true. He quotes letters, for instance, in which MacLennan carefully explains the reasons for his decision to write so directly about Canada in his novels and Cockburn clearly recognizes the difficulties of the serious novelist beginning to work in the Canada of the Thirties; he is able to illuminate such matters as the power of the first half of *Two Solitudes* with insight and economy, and indeed he has the capacity, rare among astringent critics, to praise with a force and clarity equal to that he brings to the job of condemnation. As a conservative and traditional critic, he is perhaps unusually well-equipped to discuss an essentially conservative and traditional novelist: he is sensitive to his subject's merits and defects alike, and he is uncompromisingly honest.

Cockburn's incisive study leaves us with the conclusion that by any of the normal criteria MacLennan is an ambitious and interesting but profoundly flawed novelist—a conclusion which is probably unavoidable—and further studies will have to reckon with what seems to me a definitive statement of the viewpoint of the critical tradition. What Cockburn has done is to end the first debate and clear the way for a second. After this book, it should be impossible to confuse aesthetic satisfaction with affection for a fellow-citizen. Criticism will have to look now for other qualities: it will be interesting to see what it does with the opportunity. In the meanwhile *The Novels of Hugh MacLennan* leaves the issues clearer than they have ever been. I have called Robert Cockburn uncompromisingly honest. In the last analysis, such a critic is surely the only one who can help an artist at all.

DONALD CAMERON
FREDERICTON, N.B.

CONTENTS

I	INTRODUCTION	11
II	BAROMETER RISING	29
III	TWO SOLITUDES	47
IV	THE PRECIPICE	71
V	EACH MAN'S SON	89
VI	THE WATCH THAT ENDS THE NIGHT	109
VII	RETURN OF THE SPHINX	127
VIII	CONCLUSION	145
	NOTES	157
	BIBLIOGRAPHY	161
	ACKNOWLEDGMENTS	165

CHAPTER ONE

~ INTRODUCTION

When the Jacobite Rebellion of 1745 came to an end, so did the traditional pattern of life in the Highlands. The clan system fell apart; the chiefs, previously administrators of justice, saw this prerogative pass to the Crown. The clans were forbidden to bear arms or to wear the kilt or tartan: in short, dignity was ripped from the Highlanders. In the wake of this development, the chiefs, no longer able to command the loyalty of their people, faced certain poverty; because "the value of men declined, the value of money went up." [1]

The infamous Highland Clearances became the answer to the problem. With "no resources but their land, and their land . . . encumbered by a host of unprofitable tenants," [2] the clan chiefs found a solution in the south of Scotland. Sheep were extremely profitable, but needed more grazing room than could be found on the Borders. The southern sheep-owners came to agreement with the chiefs, and the clansmen were cleared from their hills and their homes to make way for flocks of Cheviots. This deplorable situation lasted into the first half of the nineteenth century. The displaced Highlanders, crammed into emigrant ships, sailed from their homeland to North Carolina, New Zealand, Australia and Canada.

With them they brought—no doubt of this—that nameless haunting guilt they never understood, and the feeling of failure, and the loneliness of all the warm-hearted, not very intelligent folk so outmoded by the Anglo-Saxon success that they knew they were helpless unless they lived as the Anglo-Saxons did, failures unless they learned to feel (or not to feel at all) as the Anglo-Saxons ordained.

So Hugh MacLennan has written.[3] Some of his own people were driven from the parish of Kintail in the early 1800's, and they settled in Cape Breton Island. There, in Glace Bay, MacLennan was born, the child of Samuel and Katherine MacLennan on March 20, 1907. His father was a doctor, and evidently had strong influence on his son; clearly, MacLennan admired him greatly:

> He was a doctor who spent much of his earlier life in a very hard practice in a Cape Breton mining town, but thanks to his classical interests he was not isolated there. He read Latin and Greek for pleasure, he read the philosophers. In retrospect I see him as one of the least provincially minded men I ever knew, even though he was full of Scotch and Calvinist quirks. . . . My father died just before the Hitler war began, and he died knowing it was inevitable and why it was inevitable. This he understood not so much from reading the papers as from reading Thucydides.[4]

In 1913, Dr. MacLennan travelled to Europe to do research; Hugh MacLennan's only recollection of this journey is that he saw, somewhere in England, men in knickerbockers lying prone upon early aircraft which they were piloting. The family was back in Sydney when the war broke out and moved to Halifax shortly thereafter. MacLennan has written of those days in Halifax, and he tells how

> . . . my father put on the great-coat of his new uniform and went to the door and I saw the long tails of his coat blowing out behind him in the flicker of a faulty arc light as he half ran up to the corner. We heard bagpipes, and almost immediately a company of soldiers appeared swinging down Spring Garden Road from old Dalhousie. . . . my father fell in behind the last rank and faded off down the half-lit street. . . .[5]

Hugh and his mother then went to live with his grandmother in Cape Breton until about a year later, when Dr. MacLennan was "invalided home as a result of excessive work as a surgeon in the hospital."[6] From this time on, the family lived mainly in Halifax.

The young MacLennan was a fervid admirer of the Royal Navy, and knew the name, armament, and tonnage of every

British and German ship afloat. He sailed a boat in Halifax
Harbour, lived through the great explosion of 1917, and,
soon after the war, attended Halifax Academy. At this school
he had for a teacher J.W. Logan: " . . . we became conscious
that it is out of dangers that civilisations arise, and that we
lived in a province with a great tradition of culture and
adventure. The embodiment of that tradition, as I knew it,
was the senior master in the Academy, the finest teacher I
have ever known." [7] Between his father and Logan, MacLennan developed a passionate interest in the Classics:

When I was a boy in Nova Scotia I read Homer, first in
abridged translations for children, later in the original.
Although the *Iliad* was composed about a millenium before
Christ and the *Odyssey* perhaps a hundred and fifty years
later, both books seemed to me to be almost contemporary....
it required no effort of the imagination as it did with Roman
literature, with some novels laid in London, and everything written by Hans Christian Andersen, to think myself
back into the atmosphere of Homer. It was all around me in
Nova Scotia when I was young. . . . There, as in ancient
Greece, the sea and the land were linked as closely as
husband and wife. Nova Scotia captains in the last century
were known as farmer-skippers; like Odysseus, they could
lay aside a plough and then sail a ship to any quarter of the
earth.[8]

Having finished high school, MacLennan moved on to
Dalhousie University in 1925; he remembers these years as
being, on the whole, rather dull. He did have the benefit of
Logan's teaching again—he held an honorary post at Dalhousie which paid fifty dollars a year. Archibald MacMechan,
Professor of English Literature, was perhaps the major figure
there, but MacLennan does not think that he was influenced
at all by him: "I took two requisite English courses from him,
which were a picnic after the tough Classics courses. He
genuinely loved literature, but as I recall him, he was a
rather naive romantic." [9] MacLennan, who had always been
keen about sports, played basketball and tennis for his
University. He received an injury in basketball that still
bothers him, and his proficiency at tennis, which he had
begun to play at the age of 13, was such that he won the

Maritime Singles Championship; he had learned to play the game on his own, by reading Bill Tilden's books. MacLennan graduated with a B.A. in 1929, and won a Rhodes Scholarship which took him to Oxford.

When I graduated from Dalhousie in the late nineteen-twenties I knew no other part of the world beyond the province and like most Nova Scotians I had no wish to leave home. The province seemed to me to contain enough physical variety to satisfy anyone and it was linked by the direct highway of the ocean to the fountain-head of our culture. But I knew I would have to emigrate if I wanted to make a career and so did most of my classmates; it was something we all took for granted.[10]

MacLennan's Oxford college was Oriel—scene of one of his most memorable essays, "Orgy at Oriel." He thoroughly enjoyed his Oxford years. He won his Blue at tennis, played Rugby for his college, wrote poems, and travelled extensively through England and the Continent. MacLennan's tutors were Sir David Ross—"probably the most impressive Aristotle scholar of the present century," but "atrociously dull" [11]— Marcus Niehbur Tod, a kindly but distant Ancient History tutor, and E.E. Genner, who was tough on MacLennan, and helped him to get through.

Genner, in my opinion, was a great teacher and a remarkable human being. He was also a tremendous scholar with a scholarly mind like a razor's. He was generally unpopular with his colleagues because he was a strict non-conformist... But he knew men and was a great teacher. His subject was "pure classics"—i.e., Latin and Greek, and he was the Mods tutor in my time. He had come to us from Jesus where he had been senior scholar and would have become Master had he not been a dedicated teetotaller. When the Mastership fell vacant, he informed the senior common room of Jesus that if he became Master it would be his duty to wall up the wine cellar and to prohibit beer and wine in Hall. He thereupon resigned, knowing this would be unacceptable, and (came to) Oriel.[12] ... I saw him twice a week, one hour each session, man to man. And I had to prove an essay to him twice a week man to man, with no vague lecturing, no excuses possible, no chance of avoiding the assignment, no hope of bluffing through on a glib turn of phrase. Accustomed as I was to the mass-organization of a North-American university, it was a terrifying experience. There was only one way of surviving it—work like hell.[13]

In 1932 MacLennan graduated from Oxford with a Second in Honour Mods.

He came directly home: ". . . a few days after returning to Halifax from Oxford, I walked out to my old university to apply for a job; a vacancy had just been announced in my field of work, and in 1932 a new job of any kind was as rare as a snowball in August. This opening seemed to me one of those lucky chances which come rarely in life." [14] But Mac-Lennan did not get the position—he was passed over in favour of an Englishman with identical qualifications. The professor whom he saw about the matter told him, "You'd better drop the idea of teaching in Canada and go down to the States. A Canadian can always get a job there."

As I walked home that day there was a warm westerly wind blowing. It had travelled all the way up the province, and the odours of the terrain it had crossed were still in it. I could smell spruce and salt water. At that moment all my instincts were against leaving this place. I felt I had been away long enough already. I had liked England. I can truly say I had loved Oxford, as a man loves any place which is greater than its temporary inhabitants. But Oxford was through with me now. The professor's words returned to me: "You're a Canadian. You should go to the States." I realised that I had never before thought of myself as a Canadian. For in Nova Scotia—and I have since learned that it is much the same everywhere in Canada—we were Nova Scotians first and Canadians only when we applied for jobs or passports, or when a war broke out and the government wanted an army, and even then they said it was England, not Canada, that needed us.[15]

MacLennan applied for a job to every college and university in Canada, without success. That autumn he went to Princeton on a student fellowship, and enrolled in the graduate school to study Roman History. Princeton did not agree with Hugh MacLennan. He found himself constantly caught up in departmental intrigues, could never reconcile

himself to the complete separation of graduate and under-
graduate schools, and, most of all, thought Princeton too
Germanic; it was a place

. . . where all the important college buildings except one
were exact copies of famous structures in Oxford or Cam-
bridge. But the resemblance was external only. Inside they
were aseptic and modern, and what went on inside was not
what went on in any English university.
    In Canada the system of higher education is largely based
on that of the Scottish universities. Superficially, American
colleges resemble ours. But the attitude of their professors is
very different, and what they value is different. The spiritual
home of higher education in the United States, for at least a
hundred years, has been Germany.[16]

MacLennan was (and still is) of the opinion that "with
the possible exceptions of Harvard and one or two other
places, most of them small, hardly any American colleges
raise students to think, and few of them even pretend to do
so. Canadian colleges, at least until recently, *pretended* to
teach their students to think for themselves." [17]
    MacLennan graduated with a Ph.D. degree from Princeton
in 1935. Although he had not liked the university, these were
important years, for they were in large part responsible for
shaping the future course of his life. For one thing, he decided
to devote his life to writing: "During those Princeton years
I spent late hours after my academic day was over working
on a novel which was never published, always pretending I
was doing something else. I was determined to learn how to
be a professional writer." [18] This novel had a European
setting, inspired, perhaps, by interests picked up along the
way: ". . . I began studying the high priests of the new Dia-
lectic. I became acquainted with the critical writings of F.R.
Leavis, Cyril Connolly and a host of authors, including, of
course, the Master himself, who quickly found his niche as a
critic when his poetical vein ran out. Dutifully I turned my
back on the poets I had loved . . . and joined the column
that trudged off into the wasteland." [19]
    While in the United States, MacLennan travelled a good
deal, and got to know "Americans at their best, Americans
on the road. . . . truck drivers, farmers, businessmen, travel-

ling salesmen, hitch hiking unemployed, clerks leaving a girl in one town to go to a girl in another, boot-leggers and bums."[20] However, "steadily during those first three years in the United States, the knowledge was borne in on me that I did not fit. Except on the roads; anyone could fit there.... the people were not my people, nor could I become one of them."

> I missed the quietness of home. I missed the sense of my own past. I missed the knowledge that if I said something outrageous, people would not mark me down as queer, or automatically dislike me, but would make the allowances they will always make for a member of their own family, remembering that his background is also their background, and that the main part of a man is a product of it. A man needs a strange country to get a new sense of himself. But he needs his own country to be aware of his roots. Without using the phrase in the slightest sense nationalistically, I missed not being able to be a Canadian.[21]

A few months after graduating, MacLennan accepted a teaching job at Lower Canada College in Montreal; he was paid twenty-five dollars a week, but never regretted taking the position. In 1936 he married. Dorothy Duncan was an American from Chicago, and he has written of her that "It was she who helped me to discover Canada, so that I could put some of it into words; for she, in her own way, found another framework of differences when she came to live in my country."[22]

In 1936-37 MacLennan wrote another novel, this time using an American setting, but, like his first attempt, this also went unpublished. *Barometer Rising* came out in 1941, and *Two Solitudes* in 1945. In the latter year, he left Lower Canada College to devote himself entirely to writing. MacLennan had volunteered for duty at the beginning of the war, but was turned down because of a bad ear. He and his wife lived frugally during these years, their main support coming from the novels MacLennan published—*The Precipice* in 1948 and *Each Man's Son* in 1951. However, Dorothy Duncan slowly began to succumb to illness. Medical expenses were very high by 1950 and MacLennan, beset by this difficulty, started writing for magazines. Then, in 1952, he was offered a part-time position at McGill, teaching English.

By this time he was a prominent figure in Canadian letters. He had received the Governor-General's Gold Medal for Fiction in 1948 for *The Precipice,* and the same award for Non-Fiction in 1949 for his first volume of essays, *Cross-Country.* He was to win both prizes again, in 1954 and 1959, for *Thirty and Three* and *The Watch That Ends the Night.* Recognition of his importance was confirmed in 1952 when he was presented with the Lorne Pierce Gold Medal for Literature by the Royal Society of Canada; the following year he became a Fellow of the Society.

Dorothy Duncan died in 1957. Two years later MacLennan married Frances Alice Walker of Montreal. *Scotchman's Return,* his latest book of essays, was published in 1960, and *Seven Rivers of Canada* in 1961; there followed, in 1967, *The Colour of Canada* and *Return of The Sphinx.* Today, MacLennan teaches full-time at McGill, mainly, he says, "to keep in touch with the young." Montreal is now his home— he feels it to be the centre of Canadian life and the Canadian adventure. Summers he spends in a cottage in the Eastern Townships, and frequently he returns on visits to Halifax and Cape Breton. He has reconciled himself, not altogether happily, to the world in which he lives:

I became a Classical scholar just at the moment when the Classics were dropped from the educational system. . . . I worked hard to become a Rhodes Scholar, and having become one, graduated from Oxford in 1932 when only one Rhodes man in ten got a job of any kind. The only thing I learned through acquiring a Ph.D. degree was that such a degree is worthless even in the rat-race of academic job-hunting. I learned to play a lovely game called rugger, which once was the autumn sport of the Maritimes and the Pacific coast; I have lived to see it abandoned because the equipment costs too little and advertising pressures have taught Canadians to become a nation of spectators, with the result that the football they watch is played by imported gladiators. In the nineteen-thirties I had a dramatic sense and wanted to write plays, but there was no market for them in the society of that era. So I wrote six novels, four of which were published,

and when the last was finished I believed I had finally
mastered a difficult and complex art.[23]

This, of course, raises the main question under discussion
—has MacLennan in fact mastered the art of fiction? The
framework of the answer must be sought in MacLennan's
personal experience, which, undeniably, has shaped his idea
of the novel.

To begin with, there is the fact that he is, to use his own
words, "three quarters Scotch, and Highland at that." He
confesses to a Highland nostalgia, and mentions as empathetic these words spoken to him by Angus L. Mac-
Donald, then Premier of Nova Scotia: "To be a Celt is never
to be far from tears." [24] It is difficult indeed to show—with
one outstanding exception—that MacLennan's Highland
heritage has imparted any recognisable aura to his novels;
but he feels that it has. Speaking to the writer in July, 1965,
he said, *"The Watch That Ends the Night* is not an Anglo-
Saxon novel." I shall come back to this later, but I might say
here that I believe MacLennan was suggesting that his Scottish background provided a certain fire of imagination and,
especially, feeling which would otherwise have been lacking.

More easily ascertainable is the implication of the near-
epithet, "Anglo-Saxon." In the first place, MacLennan's use
of it contains an emotional inference which has its base in a
facet of Canadianism: "The Canadian's sense of his European
past," MacLennan writes, "is unique in North America. No
Americans pride themselves on where their ancestors lived
in Europe, or what they did there. Most of them don't even
know. . . . Fourth generation Canadians in Cape Breton can
tell you the name of the Highland village from which their
ancestors set out." [25] In part, this may be a slight overstate-
ment, but its meaning is clear—MacLennan's pride of blood
counts for just as much with him as his pride of country, of
which it is a part. Secondly, MacLennan has little regard for
English novelists:

Ever since 1660, it seems to me, the writers of *England*
have been on the whole more cerebral than emotional, with
a few notable exceptions. Dickens, of course, is an exception
—he wasn't half cerebral enough. But on the whole, Jane

Austen, Thackeray, Trollope (most typical of them all) and in our own century writers like Huxley, Snow, Ivy Compton-Burnett, Angus Wilson, Maugham and so many others seem deeply to distrust emotion. Even Galsworthy did, but because he *was* emotional, the result is often gross sentimentality.[26]

The same does not hold true, he goes on, for "all Anglo-Saxon American novelists. Look at Hawthorne. He disguised, but there was a volcano in his work. Melville, I presume, was Scotch." And MacLennan makes an exception for D.H. Lawrence. What he has done, then, is to set himself off from the Anglo-Saxon not only emotionally but artistically as well.

This is not to say that MacLennan applauds Scottish writers—indeed, with a very few exceptions, they inspire little applause from anyone. The paucity of good writing in Scotland he attributes to Calvinism. He is aware of similar repercussions upon Canada; however, he thinks that he has himself escaped them. And thus it is that we find him describing *The Watch That Ends the Night* as a novel that is Celtic in its inspiration and such only because it was written by a Highlander removed by four generations from Kintail to Canada.

MacLennan's early environment is another source of his individualistic stance. A Celt by inheritance, he is a Nova Scotian by birth and upbringing. This has enabled him to write with conviction and force about his native province. *Barometer Rising, Each Man's Son,* and many of his essays illustrate this allegiance. It was only after he returned from Oxford that he began to think of himself as a Canadian and not simply as a Nova Scotian.

Then there is the matter of MacLennan's largely classical education. As we have seen, his father, and J.W. Logan, his Halifax teacher, were the first to arouse in him an interest in the Classics; later, the histories of ancient Greece and Rome became subjects of study for MacLennan at each of his three universities; thus it is that much of his writing is coloured by classical allusions and comparisons. Not only do the Scottish Highlands and Cape Breton remind him of Greece, but when writing about food he recalls bizarre eating habits of the later Romans;[27] hearing the bell of a buoy in Halifax Harbour,

memories "rise like ghosts from the pit about the sword of
Odysseus." [28] Which name brings to mind George Woodcock's
essay on MacLennan's novels, "A Nation's Odyssey." He
points out the quite obvious parallel between the myth of
Odysseus and *Barometer Rising*: at the same time, however,
he goes overboard in an attempt to relate this discovery to
all the novels ". . . the Odyssey itself was the product of a
people in the process of becoming aware of itself and, appro-
priately, MacLennan uses it to illuminate the theme of
the growth of a Canadian national consciousness." [29] While
this declaration is transparently valid when applied to *Barometer Rising*, it is wrong in relation to the other five novels.
These books are coloured by the Classics, it is true, but
merely in a conventional, adjectival way. Furthermore, Woodcock compounds his mistake by claiming that MacLennan
uses throughout his novels

> a group of symbolic characters . . . the returning wan-
> derer, the waiting woman, the fatherless child, the wise
> doctor—sometimes transformed into the wise old man, and
> the primitive, violent, but essentially good giant. If we wish
> to seek a Homeric parallel, the quintet of Odysseus, Penelope,
> Telemachus, Mentor, and Eumaeus seems obvious, though
> MacLennan is too good a writer to follow the pattern slavish-
> ly, and we shall see the relationships of these five basic
> characters changing from novel to novel until, in *The Watch*
> the wanderer, the wise doctor and the primitive giant are
> finally united in that super-Odysseus, Jerome Martell. [30]

As Woodcock says, the parallel may exist "if we wish to
seek" it—this is true of many parallels. I suggest that there
are no symbolic characters outside of *Barometer Rising*, and
I do so for two reasons: first, because MacLennan himself
says, "I don't use symbols in my writing, at least not consciously"; [31] second, because I attribute the recurrence of
character types not to any intricate master-plan, but rather
to a poverty of imagination on MacLennan's part.

So far, we have followed three threads of MacLennan's
life and mentioned, if only briefly, their influence upon his
writing. Next to be considered is MacLennan's six-year
academic sojourn away from Canada. As much as he admired
England and its institutions, MacLennan came away detesting,

as he still does, the snobbery that he feels to be endemic there:

> . . . the masters of the Grand Style seldom if ever conceded in the one region where concession was required—their own hearts. A Durham could come out to Canada and help our statesmen lay the groundwork of a new kind of nation, but it never once occurred to him that independence need be a synonym for the final equality. . . . Too many of England's lovers . . . discovered with embarrassment that the love they so freely offered was not really desired, since the total acceptance of love commits an honourable man to grant a total equality in every unspoken sense of that word.[32]

MacLennan had realised at Oxford that he "knew nothing whatsoever" about his own country. It has been shown above how the Princeton years caused his national consciousness to grow; if England made him feel a stranger at times, so did the United States:

> It took me a long time to accept the fact that in the eyes of the average American this whole continent—at least all of it that is worth much—belongs to him. Americans don't realize that Canadians have the same right to feel proprietory about it that they have themselves. An American does not see the point in our assertion that we have a right to find fault with an American government, or with American big business, because what is done by his government and his businessmen profoundly affects the well-being of all Canada. The American's superiority complex, when he thinks of his country, is greater than anything the world has ever seen. His answer to our comments would probably be this: "If you want to criticise us, become an American citizen before you talk."[33]

By 1935 MacLennan had written the first of his two unsuccessful novels, and he was, as a result of his new-found Canadianism, attempting to hold England and the United States at arm's length—here is an excerpt from a letter he wrote in March, 1935 to a friend in Halifax:

> . . . I expect you will agree with me when I say that if one wants to write one must turn one's back on England altogether. Sterility is certainly the leit-motif over there and

Spender, Bottral and Auden, the latter two with their talk about "intelligence" until you go nuts listening to them, are good examples and are already ending nowhere. In the States the usual extravagance is holding them all up, and as affairs are rotten, most of their writers are swimming up and down sewers saying how tough they are. . . . I see it as my job to start in where Lawrence left off.[34]

Then came marriage to Dorothy Duncan:

It was she who showed me why the first two novels I had written were failures. I had set the scene and characters of one book in Europe, of the second in the United States. They were not authentic. The innumerable sense impressions, the feeling for country, the instinct for what is valuable in a human being—these things were all coloured by a Canadian background I had not accounted for, which neither an American nor a European would accept without an explanation that was an inherent part of the story. Few novelists, writing of contemporary life, can risk setting the scene outside their own country unless their country is known to the whole world, and unless they make one of their own countrymen the leading character. It was my wife who persuaded me to see Canada as it was and to write of it as I saw it.[35]

In October of 1941, following the publication of *Barometer Rising*, MacLennan wrote once more to his friend in Halifax:

. . . I feel that I pretty well have to sink or swim as a Canadian writer. The book before this was international in scope and in point of view, with a slightly American bias. It was no more an American novel in form and substance than *For Whom the Bell Tolls*. It was less American, because no one could possibly be more American than Hemingway. And after a long time, testing various reactions and especially my own appraisal and judgement, I came to the conclusion that a Canadian can't write authentically about the American scene. Nor is Canada important enough—yet—for a Canadian's point of view on Europe to be important. The Americans would not care, the English would not be able to distinguish it from American.

I am sure: no artist can possibly write of any society—as a base—than his own. . . . Therefore, without benefit of any background or tradition beyond what I succeed in making for myself, I seem doomed to continue.[36]

By this time, then, MacLennan's life had provided a framework that would shape his future novels: Highland Scotch, Nova Scotian, classically educated, a staunch advocate of Canadianism, and happily and fortunately married, he had, with *Barometer Rising,* marked "a major advance in Canadian fiction." [37]

Finally, it is imperative that we try to arrive at a clear picture of what, in MacLennan's opinion, a novel should be. In one of his essays, he leads off with the following paragraph:

I happen to believe that one of the most important goals in the life of the individual man is self-knowledge. I believe that the same goal is equally important for a nation. And I do not believe this self-knowledge can come, either to a man or to a country, as a gift from heaven. It is achieved by long searching, continuous study, frankness, and a willingness to look on the bad as well as the good. [38]

If one more excerpt is attached to the above, the task which MacLennan has set himself, his main purpose in writing, stands out clearly:

When one asks the eternal question, "What is Canadian Literature?" the answer seems to me to be this: It is work written about contemporary Canada by a Canadian who knows his own country and is willing to portray Canadians as they live and not as Americans and English think they live. [39]

So Hugh MacLennan's goal is to explain Canada to itself, and to the rest of the world, in terms of reality or, as he puts it, "self-knowledge." To this end he has, in each of his novels, explored various aspects of life in this country. In *Barometer Rising* his theme is the new spirit of Canadian identity which grew out of the 1914-18 War; in *Two Solitudes* the conflict between English- and French-speaking Canadians is explored; both *The Precipice* and *Each Man's Son* deal with puritanism, a shaping force in the history of the Canadian people, while the former of the two also handles the impact of the United States upon Canada; *The Watch That Ends the Night* has a theme that is essentially religious (a quest for individual self-knowledge) and therefore universal, but many sides of Canadian life, from the 1930's through the 1950's are discussed. MacLennan's latest novel, *Return of the Sphinx,* explores the continuing problems between Quebec and the rest of the country and examines the effect of the chaotic 1960's upon this nation. All of these novels, with the partial exception of *The Precipice,* are set primarily in Canada.

Virtually every critic of MacLennan has blamed him for the preponderance, and/or unsuitability, of sociological and historical data in his novels. I shall do the same. But in so doing I shall also attempt to show that MacLennan's wide familiarity with his country is not only his partial undoing as a novelist, but also, ironically, his greatest strength. And it should be pointed out that MacLennan, when he injects such material into his books, knows what he is doing; he is not being careless—simply pugnacious. Here he is clapping his hands for a man who he admits is "grossly sentimental" —John Galsworthy:

> . . . I have never been able to believe that any Englishman in the past twenty years has written a novel as true and important as *The Forsyte Saga*. It may be old hat now, but it was good hat in its time and if it is not valuable as a work of art, it is indispensable for anyone who wants to know what England was like at the end of the nineteenth century.[40]

The word that stands out in this paragraph is "important"; notice that for MacLennan his perhaps extravagant claim rests on *The Forsyte Saga*'s worth as a document rather than as an artistically successful novel. The fact may be—there are hints of this—that MacLennan sees himself more as an historian than as a creative artist.

Be that as it may, MacLennan does have very definite ideas about what a novel should be; these are principally to be found in his essay, "The Future of the Novel as an Art Form." Here he discusses the things which have sapped the novel's one-time popularity—the wealth of great fiction that already exists, the terrific output of paperbacks, the inroads made by non-fiction and television. He sees non-fiction as the novel's chief competitor because

> Ever since Lytton Strachey proved it possible to write a biography in novel form, utilizing all the tricks of the

novelist's trade, non-fiction writers have steadily been trans-
forming their art, and already they have defeated the
novelist's art in the field of accuracy. I believe that future
ages will recognise that the chief contribution made to
literary form in this century has not been made by T.S.
Eliot and James Joyce, but by writers of non-fiction. Bio-
graphies of real people used to be as dull as obituaries; now
they are fascinating. Accounts of historical and current events
used to be handled in the prose of scholars and reporters;
now they are handled with consummate art and a wealth of
artifice.[41]

However,

Non-fiction, after all, cannot entirely supplant the need for
good novels because it cannot be so intimate. . . . Non-fiction
cannot hope to give us a Hamlet, an Othello, a Natasha, an
Alyosha Karamazov, a David Copperfield. Because its subjects
are usually men and women of mark it can seldom if ever
deal successfully with the humble. If you want Sam Weller
or the old fisherman of Hemingway's book—for that matter
if you want yourself—you still must go to some form of
fiction.[42]

People have gone over to non-fiction, he explains, because
too many novels have degenerated into treatises for various
philosophies, or into banal escapism:

In the Thirties some of the most respected men in modern
fiction used the Marxist philosophy as a frame for their
stories; a few years later most of them realised that deeper
causes than any dreamed of by Marx were responsible for
the horrors of the twentieth century. Even worse is the
plight of some younger writers who have emerged since the
war. Facing a situation that frightens them, they either try
to escape it or to exorcise it. If they do the latter, they
concentrate on peripheral characters, invariably unpleasant,
whose very existence is a slap in the face to the conformist
society of the advertisers which they loathe. If they escape
it, they usually follow one of two courses. They bury a
commonplace tale about commonplace people under a
mountain of self-conscious symbolism inherited from Eliot
and Joyce, or they create a world for two in which an
ordinary boy and an ordinary girl spend the first half of the
book trying to get into bed with each other and the last half

trying to get out. Nobody can blame sensible people from turning away from these clichés.[43]

MacLennan attacks the cynicism which was so fashionable in the twenties and thirties, and which has carried over into our own time:

> I believe that the serious public has bitterly resented this automatic cynicism of so much of the recent literature it has been told to admire. Since the last war the novel, especially in the United States, has failed worst of all in dealing with the very subject in which it should excel. That subject is love.[44]

He deplores the contemporary emphasis on clinical descriptions of sex: "Inside another decade most Americans should be aware of what a naked woman looks like, and they may even prefer reality to the literary shadow." [45]

For MacLennan, "A novel's chief value lies in its capacity to entertain and in its characters. If it lacks interesting, vital and important characters, not all the style and grace in the world will prevent the public from rejecting it . . ."[46]

In order to make characters like these, the novelist must also create the backgrounds and locales in which the characters move, and make them consistent and vivid. A satisfying novel must also hold all of its characters, all of its descriptions, dialogues, ideas, arguments, scenes and actions, within a whole which is harmonious, within a whole where the surprises are seen in retrospect to have been inevitable. And in the supremely satisfying novels, as in all good works of art, there is finally a mystery.[47]

In evaluating Hugh MacLennan's novels, I shall apply the criteria he himself sets forth. It is my contention that he has never achieved in any one of his novels "a whole which is harmonious." And the major reason for this is that he, perhaps unconsciously, perhaps not, relies too heavily upon techniques which properly belong to non-fiction.

CHAPTER TWO

∼ BAROMETER RISING

Barometer Rising is, in some ways, a memorable first novel; at the same time it contains writing which is debilitating. Somehow, the book strikes a certain note of success —not because the flaws are small ones, but rather because the strengths have so much more impact.

In this novel, MacLennan is writing about three different things: the characters; Canada's quest for self-knowledge; and Halifax and its explosion of December 1917. The success of *Barometer Rising* as a work of art rests upon the author's skill in fusing these three aspects; unfortunately, he fails, and harmony and credibility are, to a large extent, sacrificed. But, strange to say, this failure does not keep the book from being remarkably entertaining and interesting—the reason being MacLennan's proficiency at creating evocative, moving, and realistic action sequences and descriptions. When one thinks back to *Barometer Rising* it is not the characters or the plot or even MacLennan's "message" that one remembers —it is, instead, the vivid recreation of the explosion and the equally memorable picture of Halifax City. And this is the aspect of the novel that will be dealt with first.

The description of the city is many-faceted; one learns not only what Halifax looks like, but why it has this appearance, what its historical background has been, how it exerts an environmental influence upon its inhabitants, and of the social customs which flourish there. In fact, too much is said about Halifax, and the book, dangerously unbalanced because of this, suffers. Paradoxically, had the space given Halifax been cut down the book would have been less enjoyable.

MacLennan has written a semi-confident defence of this seemingly careless organization:

As drama depends on the familiar, and as the social and psychological novel depends on the capacity of the public to recognise allusions, to distinguish the abnormal attitude from the normal, to grasp instantly when a character is prompted to act by the pressures of his environment and when by his own idiosyncracies, it seemed to me that for some years to come the Canadian novelist would have to pay a great deal of attention to the background in which he set his stories. He must describe, and if necessary define, the social values which dominate the Canadian scene, and do so in such a way as to make them appear interesting and important to foreigners. Whether he liked it or not, he must for a time be something of a geographer, an historian, and a sociologist, to weave a certain amount of geography, history, and sociology into his novels. Unless he did this, his stories would be set in a vacuum. He could not, as British and American writers do, take his background values for granted, for the simple reason that the reading public had no notion what they were. He must therefore do more than write dramas, he must also design and equip the stage on which they were to be played. Whether my judgment of the situation in 1939 was right or not I do not know.[1]

Undeniably, MacLennan's judgment was at fault—as was often to be the case in later novels—from an artistic stand-point. One expects characters to move through a credible and atmospheric setting; however, one does not want, or need, to be told that

The Great Glacier had once packed, scraped and riven this whole land; it had gouged out the harbour and left as a legacy three drumlins . . . the hill on which he stood and two islands in the harbour itself.[2]

or (through the supposed musing of a character) how

. . . even a landsman could see why the harbour had for a century and a half been a link in the chain of British sea-power. It is barricaded against Atlantic ground swells by McNab's Island at the mouth of the outer harbour, and by the smaller bowl of George's Island at the entrance to the stream.[3]

MacLennan's insistence on showing his setting in the smallest detail can, obviously, be disconcerting.

Generally speaking, this sort of clumsiness is all but obliterated by descriptive bits and passages which are useful in understanding the background of *Barometer Rising:* native Haligonians speak with a "clear English-sounding accent" and drink tea at every meal; the Irish, Newfoundlanders, and descendants of English garrison soldiers live in different sections of the city; descendants of Loyalists are likely to hold positions of power and are a different breed from Cape Bretoners—but self-sufficiency and stubborn pride are characteristics of most Nova Scotians; for ambitious young men Halifax is not a biding place, but for boys the harbour and its ships are fascinating. The steep, wet, nineteenth century atmosphere of Halifax is time and again captured and conveyed by MacLennan.

. . . he could hear a low, vibrant, moaning sound that permeated everything, beating in over the housetops from the sea. For a second he was puzzled; it sounded like an animal at some distance, moaning with pain. Then he realised that the air was salty and moist and the odour of fish-meal was in his nostrils. The wind had changed and now it was bringing in the fog. Pavements were growing damp and bells and groaning buoys at the harbour mouth were busy. When he reached his room in the cheap sailors' lodging he had rented that morning, he lay down, and the sounds of the harbour seemed to be in the walls.[4]

There is in this passage an appeal to the senses—one not only sees as one reads, but tastes, hears and smells. And if one is familiar with such a scene it comes all the more alive. Such atmosphere is filled out not only by Haligonians and their fixed relationship with the city, but by all the confusion and haste of war; heavy boots thunder down the cobbled streets to the wail of pipes and the harbour is alive with the shipping.

For better than half the novel—up to the explosion—Halifax itself is the protagonist. If MacLennan's intimate knowledge of his old home had not been brought forward with such evocative effect, the story would never have staggered to safety—that is, to its final third, the 1917 disaster, the most unified and by far the most powerfully written section of the book.

The explosion, when it occurs, does not come as a total surprise. MacLennan has been careful to introduce a note of tension at the beginning and this is gradually built up as one chapter succeeds another. The title itself is suggestive of impending excitement. The chapters are headed not by numerals, but by days, and most of these are punctuated by time segments. This time-bomb technique is naturally effective in creating tension. Also, from time to time, intimations of disaster are heightened by snapshots of ships in harbour: the novel covers eight days, from Sunday to Monday night; on Sunday one is told of a "freighter sliding upstream: a commonplace ship . . . ." on the Tuesday there is "a vessel flying the tricolor . . . gliding out to sea . . . and as he studied her lines and the way she was trimmed he guessed her cargo was munitions." So—expecting something "big" to happen but not knowing just what this will be nor when it will break—one is skilfully led up to the explosion, the climax of *Barometer Rising*. The "Thursday" chapter opens at 7:30 in the morning:

> . . . through this mist moved the shapes of two vessels, one a British cruiser, the other a freighter with a lean funnel and a high bow, a bulging, sordid, nondescript vessel brought to Halifax by the war.[5]

One notices here—and nowhere else in the novel—a deliberate repetition of imagery, a prophetic quality which enhances the unity of the story; the "commonplace" freighter we saw earlier is recalled as we read of this "nondescript vessel," and the ship "flying the tricolour" has now become, as it were, the *Mont Blanc*.

8:15: "There was now only one vessel moving north towards the upper harbour, the French munitions ship *Mont Blanc*." At 8:40 the *Mont Blanc* grinds into another ship; fire breaks out:

> The *Mont Blanc* had become the centre of a static tableau. Her plates began to glow red and the swollen air inside her hold heated the cargo rapidly towards the detonation point. Launches from the harbour fire department surrounded her

like midges and the water from their hoses arched up with
infinite delicacy as they curved into the rolling smoke. . . .
    Then a needle of flaming gas, thin as the mast and of a
brilliance unbelievably intense, shot through the deck . . .
near the funnel and flashed more than two hundred feet
toward the sky. The firemen were thrown back and their
hoses jumped suddenly out of control and slashed the air
with S-shaped designs. There were a few helpless shouts.
Then all movement and life about the ship were encompassed
in a sound beyond hearing as the *Mont Blanc* opened up.[6]

This passage has that sensory quality that distinguishes
MacLennan's finest descriptions. One cannot take one's eyes
off the ship—it is as if one were watching from shore through
binoculars. At the same time that we see the plates turning
red, the author is informing us of what we cannot see or
know—of the "swollen air" baking in the hold, searing the
cargo to the danger point. Then we are on our own again,
watching the bug-like fire launches swarming to the ship's
side; because of the author's prescience we know more than
the crews of the launches—we feel the need to shout a
warning. Suddenly the needle of flaming gas shoots up—
"needle," with its implications of sharp, piercing pain, is
exactly the word wanted—and our eyes follow it as it stabs
the sky. With this burst of movement, the "static tableau"
is shattered and one is momentarily with the soaking hot-
faced firemen, staggering back, feeling their helplessness and
the coarse, webbed grain of the mad, leaping hoses. With the
next sentence we are, as it were, back on shore hearing the
thin, distant futile shouts—and then the encompassing blast;
how better to describe it than with the words, "sound beyond
hearing," which convey not only its "noise," but also its
practically unimaginable power. MacLennan, then, with
admirable economy of words succeeds not only in showing
his reader the action, but makes him *feel* it, brings him into
the scene itself through a succession of images which touch
his nerve-ends.
    The ensuing narrative description is perhaps the best
which MacLennan has written. The tumult, the searing heat
of a burning city, the stench, the horror of groping in the
wreckage for bodies, the shattered crowds of the homeless,

the paralysing blizzard which strikes in the night—all these fragments, expertly fitted into the plot, bear witness to the evocative power of MacLennan's imaginative reconstruction of a singular and complicated historical event.

Any great disaster of this sort will, if capably interpreted, hold a reader's attention. But in a first-rate novel the characters should be just as believable and just as interesting as the environment and events amid which they act and think. MacLennan's characters are, with a few exceptions, never wholly believable and they are seldom interesting.

Neil MacRae is the hero. Unjustly accused of cowardice in battle in France, he has returned to try to prove his innocence. He is thought to be dead. His accuser, and commanding officer, Geoffrey Wain, has come back to Halifax ahead of him and holds a high-ranking position as Transportation Officer for the city. Penelope, Wain's daughter, is Neil's first cousin; before the war they had been lovers, and a child, whom Neil knows nothing of, had been conceived just before he had left for overseas. The other leading figure of the book is Angus Murray, a lonely, aging medical officer who has been invalided home, a man fond of the bottle—and of Penny. So there does exist the groundwork for an interesting story: will Neil recover his honour, and the woman he loves?

Unfortunately, MacRae does not come alive until the novel is half over. A pallid, shell-shocked fugitive, he shambles through the city trying to pick up clues about Wain and about the one man of his battalion who can clear him—Alec MacKenzie. Neil has little contact with anyone in the first half of the book, and because he says and does so little, one expects to understand him and believe in him through his thoughts; it is here that the most crippling aspect of the novel is revealed, the major facts of which will be dealt with below. At this point it may be said that Neil, instead of engaging our sympathy and affection, takes us on a guided tour of Halifax. Through his musings we learn about the Great Glacier, the layout of the harbour and the streets, the British influence, etc. Sometimes this internal revelation is believable, but most often one feels that Neil is reading from a MacLennan essay instead of thinking on his own; one can almost see his lips moving:

> Halifax remained much the same. It had always looked an old town. It had a genius for looking old and for acting as though nothing could possibly happen to surprise it. Battalions passed through from the West, cargoes multiplied, convoys left every week and new ships took over their anchorage; yet underneath all the old habits survived and the inhabitants did not alter. . . . The field-gun used in the past as a curfew was fired from the Citadel every noon and at nine-thirty each night. . . . The Citadel itself flew the Union Jack in all weathers and was rightly considered a symbol and bastion of the British Empire.[7]

What should be his most important recollections are about his relationship with Penny. This is purported to be a realistic novel, and no pains are spared to show Neil's intricate knowledge of Halifax; but when it comes to picturing the consummation of Neil's and Penny's love-affair, one notices MacLennan's reluctance in "equipping the stage." MacRae would, of course, have remembered more than this:

> And almost before he realised it, they had reached the hotel where he had engaged a room for the duration of his leave, and without a word she had gone in, too, and stayed with him.
> Dawn entered the room at four in the morning, the peonies stirred in a vase, and he woke. . . . She was awake, too, and they were alone in the dawn together. . . . And still they had felt no need of sleep. . . .[8]

Such half-embarrassed, half-sly references to sex were to become a MacLennan trademark. One does not demand a long, graphic description of the sexual act, but neither does one want a big CENSORED stamped across the page whenever a man and a woman get within touching distance of one another. Neil, we are told, loves Penny, has been away from her for a long, weary time, and is anxious to be with her again; in his loneliness, it is only natural that he should look forward (and backward) to her body. Regarding himself as a marked man and having secretly to seek out MacKenzie, Neil has good reasons for not going right to Penny—nonetheless, this detracts from his stature, for while he wanders the streets Angus Murray steals his fire.

Penelope is the prototype of the MacLennan heroine— mature (twenty-nine), intelligent (she designs ships), attractive (*not* beautiful), and strong-willed (but devoted to her man). She is reasonably believable, but certainly not exciting. Reacting against her hidebound father, loyally remembering Neil, or awkwardly responding to Angus Murray's advances, she becomes likeable in a humdrum sort of way. One sympathises with her in her position—a woman working in what is strictly a man's profession—and in her predicament—whether or not to forget MacRae and marry Murray. Regrettably (for the sake of the novel), one would rather see her marry the latter.

Murray is the only major character in the first part of the novel who seems fully alive and the only one who fully engages our interest and affection. Unlike Neil, he comes into contact with both Wain and Penny, and he has plenty to say. In fact he acts as a go-between for the other three main figures. It is he who informs Penny of the charges against MacRae, and it is he to whom Wain turns for help when it is learned that Neil has returned—Murray is asked to persuade him to go away and not come back. Angus's lonely but forceful character and his perceptive disillusionment with the war engages the reader and this feeling is reinforced by his sincere but futile love for Penny; he knows of her illegitimate child, but still longs to marry her. His voice has a Gaelic inflection—he comes from Cape Breton— and while he is tender and compassionate with Penny he can be blunt and uncompromising with her father and her stiff-backed, disapproving relatives. Also, he has a sense of humour. In short, Murray has various, at times colourful, qualities, and an active role. MacRae, on the other hand, is a grey, embittered avenger sliding through the background with his turgid, unreal thoughts.

This is not to say that Murray is a thoroughly credible person. In places, as we shall see, he, like Neil, is made a purveyor of the author's dogmatism and is the less believable because of this. Murray is, also, a prototype of a favourite MacLennan character—the Wise Old Man, the elderly sage.

Murray, as the story develops, passes out benevolent recommendations to Neil and Penny; also, he has been a man of skill and action in his day, is well up on his Classics and Shakespeare, and he gracefully fades out at the end of the story—these peculiarities will be mirrored by similar characters in all of the following novels. (It is worth noting as well that Murray is the first torch-bearer of a theme that MacLennan would not fully develop until *The Watch That Ends the Night:* "Last night he had relinquished the last thread of ambition which had held worries tight in his mind. But the beauty of the world remained and he found himself able to enjoy it; it stayed a constant in spite of all mankind's hideous attempts to master it." [9] The following lines give the gist of the author's belief:

The wonder of the world, the beauty and the power, the shapes of things, their colours, lights, and shades; these I saw.
Look ye also while life lasts.)

When, by the middle of the story, Neil does seek out Penny, their reunion is largely taken up by his agonising. He says that he wants her, that he's missed her, but mainly he wants to get back at her father. This obsession is understandable, but there is no satisfactory show of affection for Penny—and this, given the circumstances, seems unnatural. His harshness towards her and, when Murray appears, his condescending jealousy toward the older man, do not help; in this scene, Neil loses once and for all the chance to attain the stature with which MacLennan has chosen to invest him. While he does suddenly come to life now that he gets a chance to speak at length, what he does say does not make him at all likeable; the reader may be interested in his quest for justice but does not associate with him and, instead, resigns the great part of his understanding and sympathy to Murray.

Geoffrey Wain, whom Neil never does confront, is too obviously the villain to arouse our anger. There is nothing subtle, or original, about him; ensconced in his shipping-office, he blusters and threatens and fondles his secretary-cum-mistress—not that such a man might not *have* a mistress, but she is a shadow-figure and seems to have been included solely to increase the reader's (imagined) sense of outrage. Wain is a profiteer businessman, a black-coated, moustache-twirling antagonist. Sent home from the war for incompetence, he is depicted by MacLennan as an Anglophilic "megaloma-niac," as one of the generation "responsible for the war:" "The old men like Wain had been willing to have this war because they were bored with themselves, and now they fancied they were in control of a wonderful new age."[10] This thin declaration is never justified by the author; the closest he comes to doing so is when he has Wain think to himself that, "Here in Nova Scotia his family had gone as far as the limitations of the province permitted. He had been born at the top of things with no wider horizon to aim for; it had required nothing less than a war to better his prospects and give him a zest for advancement."[11] There were, of course, profiteers and stupid, pompous men during the 1914-18 War, but, it is an exaggeration to insinuate, as MacLennan does, that such men were "responsible" for the war.

There then are the major characters. By the middle of the novel all of them are, for the reader, flawed in one way or another. Wain is stale before he opens his mouth, Neil's tepid rambling and pained, steely eye arouse only yawns, Penny is breathing—but keeps her distance; and Murray, the most likeable and credible of the lot, is, for reasons still to be discussed, not *fully* credible.

A more happy characteristic of MacLennan's fiction is his deft touch where minor characters are concerned. One sees this apparent paradox for the first time in *Barometer Rising*. Apparent paradox, because the lesser characters are seldom portrayed by internal revelation, but, rather, by act and speech alone. Aunt Maria Wain is a case in point; she is probably more true-to-life than any other character in the book. She does not walk into a room, she stalks in, waving an I.O.D.E. banner with her voice, which "blares like a trumpet:"

"Nonsense, there's nothing the matter with you. Penelope, why weren't you in church? There was a terrible sermon." She squinted at herself in the long mirror and patted the sides of her pompadour with a pair of powerful hands. "I ran into Mrs. Taylor this evening as we came out, that woman I was telling you about in the Red Cross. She's dreadful. People like that shouldn't be allowed to take part in the war." [12]

Aunt Maria does not appear often but when she does, her flamboyant hauteur commands the scene; it is hard to believe that MacLennan did not know someone very much like her. Alec MacKenzie, with his thick Gaelic accent, his stubborn honesty, and his bewilderment in the face of a new way of life far from Cape Breton also strikes one as authentic. Penny's twelve-year old brother, Roddie, is handled effectively; he is very real indeed, with his love of the harbour and its ships; a boy in a world of his own. MacLennan himself was ten and living in Halifax in 1917 and it is apparent that, in Roddie, he is relating his own memories and reactions at the time. None of these characters is much on stage, however, and the novel, for more than half its length, is only kept alive by the descriptive analysis of Halifax, and the relationship of the characters to the city.

But a hurricane has been brewing, and when it strikes, the author—who has been sporadically dozing up to now—takes command with iron-handed confidence. Amid the tumult and the shouting of the disaster the characters find their feet and react vigorously and plausibly (except when they stop to think). Neil and Murray have spoken with MacKenzie just before the explosion and Neil is, to Murray's satisfaction and our own, cleared of the charges against him.

Half the plot is solved with the bang, for Wain—a bit too conveniently and garishly, perhaps—is found dead and naked with his secretary (with whom he's spent the night) amid the rubble. Neil and Murray react heroically, the former carrying out back-breaking rescue work and the latter, under stress, recovering his operating skills. Aunt Maria is in her glory as she turns the Wain house into a hospital and dominates proceedings with her customary verve. Roddie's boyish excitement and inquisitiveness is expertly caught. Penny, who was trapped in her office when the *Mont Blanc* blew up, has an eye badly injured—but Murray saves it. The Frasers, Penny's warmest relations, are killed in the blast; they had adopted Penny and Neil's child, which survives and is re-united with its parents in the end. These action sequences of the last third of the novel, coupled with MacLennan's descriptive ability, comprise a convincing and memorable piece of writing. Whenever he has to show people in strenuous physical activity MacLennan is at his best. He has projected himself into their place, he knows instinctively how men will perform in a demanding galvanic situation. Furthermore, in view of what we know about their natures, the characters perform logically. Murray had resolved him-self to his loneliness just before the holocaust and his courage follows this self-recognition; Neil's courage—the basis of his torment—is decisively proven and he is shown to be a natural leader, which we had, without much caring, expected to be the case all along. Penny, not surprisingly, bears up stoically under pain.

If Halifax was the protagonist in the first part of *Barometer Rising*, the explosion and its effects hold the same position in the last part; the story survives because of this vivid, documentary reconstruction.

The parallel between the novel and the Odysseus myth is borne out by the ending, where Neil says:

"Wise Penelope! That's what Odysseus said to his wife when he got home. I don't think he ever told her he loved her. He probably knew the words would sound too small."

So Neil regains his honour and his lover and can look to the future hopefully and with new-found confidence.

But this reunion is not as simple as it sounds. There is, unfortunately, another side to the use of this myth, the fact that, as George Woodcock has said, MacLennan uses it as a vehicle for the theme of "the growth of a Canadian national consciousness." The omnipresence of this theme shatters what artistic merits the novel has just as effectively as the explosion had levelled Halifax. If one examines the novel from a stylistic viewpoint, MacLennan's use of theme is seen to be catastrophic on three separate but closely interwoven counts: artistic intent, characterisation, and space.

First of all, where *intent* is concerned, MacLennan has

failed to live up to his own criteria: "A novel's chief value lies in its capacity to entertain and in its characters. If it lacks interesting, vital and important characters, not all the style and grace in the world will prevent the public from rejecting it." The trouble is, that the author's intent is always in doubt—one comes away from the novel feeling that he was more interested in laying down an idea that obsessed him than in drawing real people. Concomitantly, far too much *space* is given over to this message; the reader is bludgeoned into scowling semi-passivity by pages full of heavily italicised lectures on the Meaning of Canada. And, worst of all, these lectures are read to us by the *characters* through what are purported to be their inner thoughts. This is "the most crippling aspect" of the novel that was mentioned above in connection with Neil and Murray. Had MacLennan developed this theme through dialogue, through spoken comment and discussion, the problem would probably not have arisen—at least it would have been natural within the context of the novel.

The only way in which to illustrate this debility is to give a few pertinent excerpts; it can then be seen how the essayist, the non-fiction man, has shoved the novelist aside. Neil, a transparent representative of this new Canadianism, is made to think:

The life he had led in Europe and England in these past two years had been worse than an emptiness. It was as though he had been able to feel the old continent tearing out its own entrails as the ancient civilisations had done before it. There was no help there. For almost the first time in his life, he fully realised what being a Canadian meant. It was a heritage he had no intent of losing.[13]

(Geoffrey Wain, in keeping with his dark role, exclaims. "Everything in this damn country is second-rate. It always is, in a colony.")

Murray, waiting for Penny to appear at one point in the novel, "thinks":

. . . Halifax, more than most towns, seemed governed by a fate she neither made nor understood, for it was her birthright to serve the English in time of war and to sleep neglected when there was peace. It was a bondage Halifax had no thought of escaping because it was the only life she had ever known; but to Murray this seemed a pity, for the town figured more largely in the calamities of the British Empire than in its prosperities, and never seemed able to become truly North American.[14]

Penny cogitates:

Living in a great nation virtually guaranteed by the United States, the present crop of publicists seemed determined to convince Canadians that their happiness would be lost forever if they should aspire to anything higher than a position in the butler's pantry of the British Empire.[15]

Indeed, this patriotism is never far from their thoughts. Neil, stumbling through the snowy, smouldering ruins of the city on rescue work, is assigned the following rumination:

He had come home and seen his city almost destroyed, yet he knew beyond any doubt that the war was not all powerful. It was not going to do to Canada what it had done to Europe. When it ended, there would be madness in the Old World. Men would be unable to look at each other without contempt and despair. . . . The war might be Canada's catastrophe, but it was not her tragedy; just as this explosion in Halifax was catastrophic but not tragic. And maybe when the wars and revolutions were ended, Canada would begin to live . . . would herself pull Britain clear of decay and give her a new birth.[16]

Murray again:

We're the ones who make Canada what she is today, Murray thought, neither one thing nor the other, neither a colony nor an independent nation, neither English nor American. And yet, clearly, the future is obvious, for England and America can't continue to live without each other much longer. Canada must therefore remain as she is, non-committed, until the day she becomes the Keystone to hold the world together.[17]

MacLennan is adamant. As the story draws to its close, Neil is still labouring the point:

Why was he glad to be back? It was so much more than a man could ever put into words. It was more than the idea that he was young enough to see a great country move into its destiny. It was what he felt inside himself, as a Canadian who had lived both in the United States and England. Canada at present was called a nation only because a few laws had been passed and a railway line sent from one coast to the other. In returning home he knew he was doing more than coming back to familiar surroundings. For better or for worse he was entering the future, he was identifying himself with the still-hidden forces which were doomed to shape humanity as surely as the tiny states of Europe had shaped the past. Canada was still hesitant, was still hamstrung by men with the mentality of Geoffrey Wain. But if there were enough Canadians like himself, half-American and half-English, then the day was inevitable when the halves would join and his country would become the central arch which united the new order.[18]

So, as Neil stands there, on the last page of the book, whispering sweet nothings to Penny, his mind is elsewhere, "identifying . . . with the still-hidden forces."

In view of the above passages—tedious, thickly emotional, completely unrealistic—it is hard to understand how Edmund Wilson could write the following with a straight pen: "There is . . . a parable in *Barometer Rising,* but not preached about or allowed to grow maudlin, as in some of his other novels."[19] If we examine the definition of the term "parable" we see why Mr. Wilson is mistaken. "A parable is a short narrative, presented so as to bring out the analogy, or parallel, between its elements and a lesson that the speaker is trying to bring home to us."[20] As has been shown above, Neil (and Angus and Penny to a lesser extent) represents a new Canadian outlook, that is, the "lesson;" he is deeply concerned about Canada's outdated and humbling reliance on Great Britain and he knows that his country must, if it is to attain self-knowledge and individuality, become "half- American and half-English." The parallel between the elements is contained not only in Neil and the Anglophilic Wain, but in Halifax as well, with its lingering, somewhat tired traditions. This much is clear. Where the trouble lies is in the vehicle of this lesson—a novel which is intended to be realistic, characters and all. The parable is driven home at the expense of the characters and it simply does not fit harmoniously into their thoughts—because they do dwell on it at such length, it becomes a discordant element. It *does* grow maudlin; it is, no matter how sincere, in the form of uncontrolled emotional pleading—and the book, as an artistic creation, is crippled by it.

This discordant element pervades the novel from beginning to end; one is made uncomfortable by the idea that the explosion is being used merely as a gigantic purge to cleanse Halifax (Canada) of her old "insecurity." There is this intention, as we have noticed above, but it is mercifully overshadowed by the author's interest in the detail of the disaster, by his vivid creation of scenes and action in the last one hundred pages. MacLennan himself has written that "In *Barometer Rising* the background is the most essential part of the book. The plot is melodramatic. . . ."[21] In melodrama, "the credibility of . . . character . . . is sacrificed for violent effect, in a drama contrived according to an emotional opportunism;"[22] such, regrettably, is the case here.

The novel over—Wain obliterated, Murray having faded away, and Neil and Penny arm-in-arm, rather like communal workers in a Russian subway painting out to build a better State—the novel over, we can summarize our impressions of the characters. Penny was never warm enough or forceful enough to capture and hold our interest; Murray was, but in spite of all he had going for him, he was rendered partly unbelievable by his creator—one admires him, but at the same time one is always conscious of the fact that he's been drugged into parroting the author's message; as for Neil—the hero, mind you—he is, except when he's allowed to go off on rescue work, a robot who spews statistics, registers self-pity and anguish (but never humour), and announces at regular intervals manifestoes on Canadianism. These characters are hardly, to use MacLennan's own criterion, "more real than the reader's personal friends."

In summarizing *Barometer Rising* one must return to the matter of the three major aspects of the novel, the theme, the background, and the characters, and to the question of how competently fused they are. The answer is that they're hardly fused at all. Harmony does not exist. Strong points would be the background of setting and historical recon-

struction, men in action, a plausible and reasonably interesting plot, the structure, and most of the minor characters.
Always tearing at these strengths are those glaring weaknesses, those unintentional demolition experts, the major
characters with their lectern-pounding gospel.

Barometer Rising may be seen as a premonitory work,
first-rate in some respects, clumsy and unconvincing in others.
It is significant that its power and its disjointedness are the
results largely of techniques that are the province of the
essayist or of the historical novelist. Finally, there is a
"mystery"—not, however, the sort which MacLennan sees as
a criterion for a successful novel; the mystery is that Barometer Rising wins through in the end, that people do remember having read it: "Oh, yes—that's the book about the
Halifax Explosion, isn't it?" This long-range impact of the
book may be likened to that enjoyed by Lytton's Last Days
of Pompeii. Let the author have the last word: "The book is
more a tour de force than a novel; when I wrote it I regarded
it as an experiment. It amazes me to hear from time to time
that it is still in demand, though the amazement is not un-
tempered with pleasure." [23]

CHAPTER THREE

∽ TWO SOLITUDES

THE TITLE of MacLennan's second novel has long since passed into the language as a common descriptive phrase of Canadians; and *Two Solitudes* is probably still the best-known of his books. MacLennan wrote it, one feels certain, because of the importance of the theme; here was a chance to examine the major rift in Canadian life; here, conco-mitantly, was the chance for MacLennan to establish himself solidly in the role of sociological historian, of spokesman, as it were, for Canada. Edmund Wilson has written that

> Mr. MacLennan seems to aim . . . to qualify, like Balzac, as the "secretary of society," and one feels that in his earnest and ambitious attempt he sometimes embarks upon themes which he believes to be socially important but which do not really much excite his imagination. An example of this, it seems to me, is . . . *Two Solitudes.*[1]

On the contrary, one feels that MacLennan's imagination was excited by the theme—the first part of the book surely proves this—but that he fails to find enthusiastic critical approval rather because he refused to make a conscientious effort at sustained artistry. There is a suggestion to support this idea in an essay of the author's:

> . . . I published at the height of the King era a book called *Two Solitudes* which sold more copies in Canada than any Canadian novel since *Maria Chapdelaine.* Literary merit had no connection with this sale; the book merely happened to put into words what hundreds of thousands of Canadians felt and knew.[2]

[47]

MacLennan seems almost to be daring us to attach too much importance to "literary merit"—instead, we are meant to applaud because he got his message over, loud and clear. But, after all, since MacLennan has chosen to deliver his nationalistic campaign through the medium of fiction, he has to be judged as a craftsman. While the over-all impression left by *Two Solitudes* is perhaps more disappointing than that imparted by *Barometer Rising*, MacLennan has, to a great extent, improved his technique. And there is no denying that this novel said, in 1945, a number of things which the average Canadian reader was himself too inarticulate to express; in its day, *Two Solitudes* came as both a revelation and a confirmation of a situation—the French-English problem—that was, and still is, significantly and importantly Canadian. The title is drawn from Rainer Maria Rilke:

> Love consists in this,
> that two solitudes protect,
> and touch, and greet each other.

The story begins in 1917 in the riverside parish of Saint-Marc, Quebec. Almost immediately the plot takes shape; it develops through personal conflicts among major characters, conflicts which mirror the French- vs English-Canadian predicament.

Athanase Tallard is the protagonist of the first half of the novel. He comes of a long line of anti-clerical seigneurs, is better educated and far wealthier than anyone else in the parish, and is the local M.P. Despite his disenchantment with the power wielded by his church, he is proud of his heritage and of his own people; he has been frustrated by his failure to help them move ahead, before it is too late, into a new, steadily progressing world. The conscription crisis is raging, and Tallard is in favour of full mobilization.

Vehemently opposing him is Father Beaubien, the parish priest. He is proud of having, through his own efforts, built the largest church for forty miles around: "It was larger even than the largest Protestant church in Montreal where million-aires were among the parishioners. And Saint-Marc num-bered less than a hundred and thirty families." Beaubien is sincere, but a simple man and in many ways a narrow-minded one: "Quite literally he believed that God held him accountable for every soul in the place." He epitomises both the weakness and the strength of the Roman Catholic clergy in Quebec; it is through men such as himself that the Church controls the population—yet he stands for a more traditional, and probably happier, way of life than that which is encroaching from the outside. Saint-Marc is cut off from the main current of world and national affairs, and the priest wants things to remain that way: "Let the rest of the world murder itself through the war, cheat itself in business, destroy its peace with new inventions and the frantic American rush after money. Quebec remembered God and her own soul, and these were all she needed." [3] Beaubien is against the war and defies conscription. So there is, first of all, a conflict between these two men; Tallard aligns himself with the wider world of national responsibility while Beaubien stands for narrow provincialism.

Tallard brings two English Canadians to the village. John Yardley is a retired Nova Scotian sea-captain and a Protestant. Huntly McQueen, shrewd and calculating, is "rapidly becoming one of the richest men in Canada," and represents, in the novel, the Scots-Canadian businessmen who control Quebec Province from Montreal: "Being an Ontario Presbyterian, he had been reared with the notion that French Canadians were an inferior people, first because they were Roman Catholics, second because they were French." Yardley decides to buy a farm and stay on, and McQueen broaches the idea of building a power dam on a local river—it would bring in a factory, which in turn would produce revenue for the debt-ridden parish. Beaubien opposes both moves: he regards factory towns as beds of sin and intends to keep his people on the land, and he has no use for "English" men: "No English Canadian had ever owned land in this parish." Tallard, who has heretofore only seen the proposed location of the dam as a scenic spot, and who distrusts businessmen of McQueen's stripe, is nevertheless attracted to the proposition because it promises a chance for his people to develop their own resources. Also, however, he spots a personal opportunity. The site is on his property and, feeling his career in parliament to be a failure, he sees a chance to make a name, money, and a new position for himself.

In less than twenty pages MacLennan has established the thematic framework of his novel by showing the numerous antagonisms inherent in such a situation: French against English; Catholic against Protestant; Quebec against Montreal; old against new. Tallard, his priest, and McQueen are caught up in a maelstrom of differences and Yardley will be trapped in the middle.

Tallard has two sons, Marius, by his first wife, and Paul, by his second wife, Kathleen. Paul, in the first half of the novel, is just a boy; largely ignored by his father, he is comforted by, and becomes a close friend of, Yardley. In the full course of the book, however, he and his brother come to enact on a different level the same conflict that besets their father and priest.

Marius is a university student and a Quebec nationalist. Like Father Beaubien, he loathes the British and is an unswerving Catholic. Rifling his father's desk, he comes across some writing criticising the Church. He regards this as heretical and considers his father not only a traitor to his race for his stand on conscription, but now a traitor to his religion as well. Jansenism, puritanical Catholicism, is the trouble with Marius; his nature is secretive, and he feels himself to be an outcast within his own family. Kathleen, who is not much older than himself, he both resents for superseding his own mother, a nun-like woman, and desires for her beauty. But Tallard, whose time has largely been given to politics, must share the blame for Marius' attitude; he has not been a companion to his sons and is, for all his logic and intelligence, a distant, rather cold man. This lack of parental consideration has spurred Marius' alienation.

We see Marius at a political rally in Montreal, howling against conscription, his ego inflated by applause. Accused by an English soldier of being a "yellow son of a bitch," Marius smashes him to the ground and goes into hiding "to keep out of the army in order to defy the English and assert his rights as a French Canadian. And he would be doing even more than that. He was saving himself for his career,

a career that he knew now would be a crusade." Thus, depth
is added to the already internecine atmosphere of the plot.
Tallard's wife, Kathleen, provides yet another conflict
within the story. She hates Saint-Marc. Of Irish descent, she
comes from Montreal and her main desire is to live there
again. Saint-Marc regards her as a foreigner and condemns
her "for not having a child a year." The marriage of Tallard
and Kathleen is a very weak link in the plot. She comes of a
working-class background, has had no education to speak of,
and has held jobs as a salesgirl and a hat-check girl "in one
of the fashionable hotels." Sex was her favourite extra-
curricular activity and Tallard met her in bed, and "to her
surprise" asked her to marry him when his first wife died.
This strikes one as being extremely improbable when the
contrasting social backgrounds of the two are taken into
consideration. MacLennan never satisfactorily explains Tallard's infatuation; it is suggested that Kathleen's "lush body"
is the only reason.

Kathleen's apparent purpose in the novel is to make Paul
half- "English." She is successful there. Also, she adds another
dimension to Tallard's dilemma. Kathleen figures in the
weakest episode of the first part of the book, a love-making
scene with a returned army major. One sees here how
easily MacLennan falls, when discussing sex, into the
romantic clichés of the women's magazines:

"You're miraculous! Are you always like that?"
"Are you?"
"No."
"I'm not either."
etc.[4]

Such clumsy writing makes a sham of MacLennan's preten-
sions to realism and, of course, forms a hollow spot in what
is, for the most part, an interesting and convincing story.

Father Beaubien learns of Tallard's "heretical" writing
from Marius, and eventually takes him to task on this score
and also for his "failure" in having only two children. In
one of the best scenes in the book, Tallard is confronted by
the priest in his library. The latter's narrowness is painful
to read about: prints of Voltaire and Rousseau he mis-

takes for family portraits, and he distrusts the many English books on the shelves. But this ignorance is countered by his insight into Tallard's character. They discuss Marius and Beaubien asks, "Have you ever shown a father's natural feeling toward him? Have you ever really gone out of your way to help him?" Tallard has decided to send Paul to an English school so that he'll learn to mix naturally with English boys and so he can get a scientific education. Beaubien insists upon a French, Catholic school and flays Tallard for backing "materialism" and war.

Shortly afterwards, Marius, bitterly cynical and on the run, returns and goes into hiding. In the ensuing confrontation the fanatical priest threatens Tallard, who has refused to back down on the factory scheme, with a disclosure that shocks and weakens the older man: Marius has known, and this we now see to be the underlying cause of his rebellion, that on the night of his mother's death his father slept with Kathleen in a hospital room near that containing the body.

Marius is captured and taken off to the army. An informer, Janet Methuen, gave him away; she is Lardley's daughter, and turns informer because her husband has died fighting in France. Also, and more importantly, she is an agent, and a victim, of her social background; having married into the English "aristocracy" of Montreal, she has been trained to despise the French. Yardley remonstrates with her and she replies: "It makes me furious, all this pampering of them. It's time they were brought to heel." Beaubien taunts Tallard with what has happened and with having let Paul, who has been their companion on their vacations, associate with Janet's young daughters. He demands that Tallard, once and for all, dismiss the plan for the factory—if he refuses, his name will be read out in church; every voter in his constituency will know that he is condemned.

The outcome is tragic and manifold: the Tallard family is ostracised in Saint-Marc, and Kathleen turns upon her husband, accusing him of being an old fool. He and Paul join the Presbyterian Church in Montreal, and the family moves to the city. As Part One (1917-1918) of the novel ends, Tallard is hanging on to his final shred of hope—that the factory will be built and that the money from it will vindicate him, in his own eyes and Kathleen's.

With Part Two (1919-1921) the first half of the novel finishes in a satisfactorily inevitable fashion. The last meeting between Tallard and McQueen is convincingly portrayed. They were to have been partners in the factory scheme but now McQueen has backed out—he refuses to go ahead with plans in conjunction with a man toward whom Saint-Marc is antagonistic. In reply to Tallard's furious protests that this will mean his ruination, McQueen answers: "Come, Tallard, be reasonable. You French-Canadians make too much trouble for yourselves—far too much." Tallard is broken, bewildered, and embittered:

> He remembered a sentence of McQueen's and gave it a different twist: "The tragedy of French-Canada is that you can't make up your minds whether you want to be free-thinking individuals or French-Canadians choosing only what you think your entire race will approve . . ." Like all you English, free with advice! But do they ever help a man? Do they ever stretch out a hand? Do they ever really want us to have a chance? [5]

Three years pass, and Tallard dies. On his deathbed he calls for a priest and returns to his Church. Marius, a law-student now, is jubilant. His young brother is confused, and as Athanase breathes his last, Marius and Kathleen fight for possession of Paul. Kathleen wins, and the first half of *Two Solitudes* closes with her and her son in a cramped Montreal apartment. Tallard has died bankrupt.

The plot of the first half of *Two Solitudes* is, despite a few flaws, extremely convincing and satisfactory. This is because the plot and its characters contain the theme within themselves. It is through the actions and personalities of the characters that the theme becomes clear; and the plot develops logically out of these actions and the natures which incite them.

Tallard, we realise, is a man caught between two views of life, each of which is pulling him in a different direction. He scorns his Church, yet he returns to it in the end; he is repelled by McQueen, but he can't help envying the wealth and progress for which the man stands; he loves Saint-Marc and its old ways, yet he is certain that it is his duty to radically alter the tempo and flavour of the parish. MacLennan handles internal revelation far more competently in this novel than he did in *Barometer Rising*. Thematic ideas are contained principally in dialogue, rather than in contemplation, and thus become far more credible and vital. Tallard's debates and conversations with Beaubien, McQueen, and Yardley are heavily weighted on the thematic side, but, when one takes into account the circumstances of the plot, this is not objectionable. Here, for example, is Tallard speaking to Yardley:

"The trouble with this whole country is that it's divided up into little puddles with big fish in each one of them. I tell you something. Ten years ago I went across the whole of Canada. I saw a lot of things. This country is so new that when you see it for the first time, all of it, and particularly the west, you feel like Columbus and you say to yourself, 'My God, is all this ours!' Then you make the trip back. You come across Ontario and you encounter the mind of the maiden aunt. You see Methodists in Toronto and the Presbyterians in the best streets of Montreal and the Catholics all over Quebec, and nobody understands one damn thing except that he's better than everyone else. The French are Frencher than France and the English are more British than England ever dared to be. And then you go to Ottawa and you see the Prime Minister with his ear on the ground and his backside hoisted in the air. And Captain Yardley, you say God damn it!" [6]

MacLennan has said that this is "a passage which dozens of strangers mentioned when they wrote to me about the book." [7] Obviously, MacLennan was able to put into words what a great many Canadians felt but were unable to define; and, generally speaking, such material is fitted—as here—effectively into the pattern of the first half of the novel.

Tallard is by no means simply a vehicle for the theme. One sees him to be driven by his own nature, by his sense of family pride and his disillusionment in not having lived up to his own expectations. He has lost his first wife, whom he loved deeply but whose aversion to sex he deplored, and

finds himself, when we come to the novel, too old and staid
to satisfy Kathleen. Politically, he has never attained high
rank, and his career—as well as his second wife—has aliena-
ted him from his sons. He is hurt by the parish's rejection of
him, however his growing bitterness is not directed only
against them but against himself as well. He stands to make
a fortune by the factory, and thus his scorn for both his
priest and his business partner is mixed with guilt. Because
we understand Tallard's temperament we believe in these
divisive conflicts.

He is a man beset by many dilemmas, all of which
combine to crush him in the end. Like Hamlet he is inde-
cisive; like Lear he wrecks his own family life and the order
of his "state"—for McQueen goes on to build the factory
alone, and Saint-Marc is transformed; like Michael Henchard
he is a victim of his own environment; there is something of
Prospero about him, too: through the life he plans for Paul—
partially, one must remember, out of selfish motives stemming from divided loyalties—he hopes that, one day, there
will be reconciliation and new hope. Clearly, Tallard is a
tragic figure; flawed by pride, a vacillating sort of stubborn-
ness, and ambitious but well-meaning gullibility, he falls
from fortune to misery and is wiped out. Certainly his mis-
fortune is more than he deserves, and we are moved to pity.
Do we, however, consider him a tragic *hero?* How much
"greatness" is there in Tallard? and how much "goodness?"
Unfortunately, there is little, if any, of either. He is the outstanding figure in *Two Solitudes,* and is very real—but, like
most of MacLennan's heroes, he is too much given to self-
pity and to an almost painfully sincere sense of purpose.
Where one looks for stoic humour or strength there is only
bitterness, irresolution, and weakness. One sympathises with
Tallard, one understands him and hopes for him—but one
neither likes nor admires him.

The sympathy that is generated for him derives from the
actions not so much of himself as of others; one is reacting
against McQueen, Beaubien, Marius and Kathleen instead
of for Tallard. From a technical standpoint he unifies the
first half of the book. It is because of the relationships that

others have with him that the plot develops, and with it the theme. Each of the other major characters gains importance and holds our interest mainly because of his involvement with Tallard.

This is true of Huntly McQueen. His relationship with Tallard resembles, in several ways, Donald Farfrae's association with Henchard. In each case a cold, practical businessman is brought into a backwater; his up-to-date, progressive ideas shatter the old order, and the main representative of that order gets caught up in a predicament of his own making, cannot cope, and eventually is driven, broken and penniless, to his death.

The minute McQueen saw the falls of Saint-Marc he thought of power and profit; Tallard had seen them all his life and only thought them beautiful. McQueen respects Tallard's authority, but sums him up as being "probably a poor businessman." To Athanase, McQueen belongs to that class in Montreal on whom dollars grow "like barnacles; and their instinct for money was a trait no French-Canadian seemed able to acquire."

MacLennan's explanation of his background contributes greatly to our belief in McQueen's character. The fat son of poor Presbyterians, he came up the hard way—on the Bible and on beatings at his school. His intelligence carried him through university, after which he inherited a dying business and made it flourish. Discovering that he had this flair, he devoted his life to business. Aside from being a trustee in the Presbyterian Church he has virtually no outside activities; money is an end in itself, an end justified by his nightly prayers for his dead, strict mother; he is unmarried and "no woman with a bosom could be quite a lady in his eyes." Tough and unscrupulous, he is so dedicated to his way of life that he believes himself to be a fair and honest man. His moral values and his business "ethics" are practically one and the same thing.

McQueen has, because of his wealth and financial acumen, been accepted almost as an equal by Montreal's social elite; he moves among his fellow barons of St. James Street comfortably and is taken into the confidence of leading

Westmount families. It is when one sees McQueen in his own particular environment that he becomes especially life-like. In *Barometer Rising* one couldn't take Geoffrey Wain seriously because he was too "flat" a character—one never sufficiently understood why he acted as he did nor what he was really like. McQueen is, in a sense, a rounded, believable Wain; the reader knows his early background and his present one, is a party to his thoughts, and sees his special brand of reasoning develop and take form in action. MacLennan forces us not only to detest McQueen, but also to give him our grudging respect.

One may not respect Marius, but, again, one finds him a thoroughly convincing figure. His fanaticism is a logical development of his dedication to his saintly mother; of the "traumatic shock" he suffered that night in the hospital; of his father's unintentional rejection of him; and of the disturbing, sensual presence of Kathleen. The end result of these factors is Marius' alliance with Beaubien and the subsequent action. Marius is not a simple, flaming separatist, but a young man reacting in a realistic manner to psychological and environmental influences. His cynical disillusionment, hypocrisy, and misguided sincerity and dedication all help to make him a solid, living presence.

MacLennan deals briefly with Beaubien's early life—enough so that we find his beliefs and actions a natural element of the context. His simple, one-sided personality would not hold up were it not for the fact that one is always aware of his power; he shows himself a good judge of human nature, speaks with vitality, and his presence is constantly reflected, even when he is not on the scene, in the conversations and contemplations of other characters, minor and major—notably Tallard.

Janet Methuen is just as real in her way as Beaubien is in his. She is neurotic, misguided, and singularly unpleasant. Once more, this can be explained by her background. Having married into Town of Mount Royal society from more humble origins, she has been twisted by her desire to live up to unfamiliar but socially desirable standards. Early on, her nature was being moulded into a sort of conformity that

MacLennan detests: "Her voice was a clipped imitation of the British. The Englishwomen who had run the finishing school to which her mother had sent her had done all they could to prevent her from talking or thinking like a Canadian." Barely thirty, she is lean and severely English in dress and appearance. She rations herself on food, is willing to go hungry "to make herself feel worthy of the British." In the first half of the novel Janet serves a triple purpose: her young daughters meet Paul at Saint-Marc; she betrays Marius, thus giving impetus to Tallard's ouster from the parish; and she, along with McQueen, enables MacLennan to deal in considerable depth with a branch of society that is just as distinctively Canadian as the parish on the Saint Lawrence.

The above characters are successful; one believes in them, finds their actions and beliefs the logical result of their environments and natures. There are, however, two characters who are not fully believable and who do not fit comfortably into the first-half context—Kathleen and Yardley.

Kathleen, we have already noted, is a bizarre choice for Tallard to have made. This awkwardness might have been partially overcome had MacLennan invested her with some sort of distinction, or at least force. But she is a phantom-figure and never comes alive. About all one knows about her is that she is too young for Tallard, out of place in his home, and self-centred and aloof in her relationships with other human beings, including her son.

Nor can one reconcile oneself completely to Yardley's presence in the novel. Taking into account his nautical life, MacLennan has endowed him with an artificial leg and a flow of witticisms uttered in the Maritime vernacular. It is hard to believe that such a man would choose Saint-Marc as his home; but he wants to be near his daughter, and an old ship-mate of his hailed from the parish—this we are meant to take as sufficient justification for his removal to a hot-bed of French-Canadian Catholicism.

Nonetheless, his role is clear. He is, because of his down-East background, able to view the Quebec situation with detachment; he is the chorus of the tragedy. As such, his

comments are usually valid and helpful in illuminating the
theme. Where the trouble comes in is in his personality.
Despite his salty and often ungrammatical dialect he is given
to reading Shakespeare and to playing chess; he is kindly,
benevolent, and always has the right answer, is the second of
a line of "sages" in MacLennan's novels. Besides acting as
the chorus, he becomes a second father to Paul and moulds
him, as best he can, to his own far-seeing, non-fanatical
attitude. When the novel moves into its second half, Yardley,
having left Saint-Marc, seems much more acceptable; but
stumping his hearty way about the parish he strikes a jarring
note.

If Yardley represents the homespun Maritimer, Major
Dennis Morey, the man who sleeps with Kathleen, is the
Spirit of the West. He praises Winnipeg to the skies, and
one suspects that he was included as a "filler" to build up
the over-all image of Canada for the reader. Also, he may
have had a few talks with Neil MacRae in France:

". . . Canada isn't England, and too many Canadians try
to pretend it is, generally they're the rich ones, and they pay
the money and make the choices. Does our Western prairie
look like anything in England, for God's sake? Then why
try to cover it with English architecture?" He shrugged his
shoulders. "After a while they'll get another idea. They'll
pretend we're exactly the same as the States. And they'll
start to imitate ideas from down there. But is there anything
in the States like the Saint Lawrence Valley? For that matter,
is there anything in the States like us—the collective us?" [8]

This has the familiar ring of the MacLennan lecture, but it
is rendered credible by being expounded in the course of
conversation.

It can be seen, then, that the majority of the leading
characters unify and illuminate, through their personalities,
and actions, the plot and the theme. The awkward, unsure
treatment of theme so noticeable in *Barometer Rising*, has,
except for a few minor recurrences, disappeared in the first
half of *Two Solitudes*. While the characters do, of course,
symbolise divisive elements in the Canadian population, they
are by no means simply vehicles for MacLennan's opinions.
We can see, as we read, why there is distrust on one side

and condescension on the other, why the problem is so intricate and explosive. But at the same time we have an affinity with the actors and are caught up in the tragic course of their lives.

Another major strength, and one tightly interwoven with the single unity of characterisation, plot, and theme, is the setting. We move, for the most part, between Saint-Marc and Montreal. The leisurely, time-honoured pace of life in the parish is memorably portrayed: Polycarpe Drouin's general store with its jumble of merchandise and perpetual checker games; Tallard's house, "built by the first member of the family who came to Canada in 1672;" the local customs and the local characters—all make a lasting impression on the reader. MacLennan draws these scenes with affectionate honesty. He also captures the spirit of Montreal, and there are fine general descriptions of that city. But, because he is dealing with Montrealers such as McQueen and Janet, these pictures of a locale and its special life are often satire:

It was a huge stone house on the southern slope of Mount Royal. Harvey Methuen's family was decidedly rich, the money coming from government bonds and stocks in breweries, distilleries, lumber, mines, factories and God knew how big a block of Canadian Pacific. It was a large family and every branch of it lived in stone houses with dark rooms hung with wine-red draperies, and they all had great dark paintings on their walls framed in gilded plaster.[9]

Here is a snapshot of Paul's school in the city:

. . . the school bowed heads for a short prayer and then stood at attention and sang *God Save the King*, looking up to the picture of King George, draped with the Union Jack, their eyes lighting at the same time on the large group-photograph that also hung behind the platform, containing the picture of . . . the men who formed the guiding committee of the board of governors.[10]

The boys never worried themselves about national problems of any sort; indeed, they did not know they existed. Their home was the English section of Montreal; as a result of what everyone told them, their country was not Canada but the British Empire.[11]

Sociological information, one sees, is effectively conveyed
through such descriptions. MacLennan's sympathies, it is
plain, do not lie with England. One wonders, however,
whether such criticism of Canada in 1917-1921 is helpful or
even meaningful. She was a young country, and it was only
natural, given her history, that she should identify with Great
Britain—it is only very recently that Canada has come to
grips with the problem of self-knowledge. On the other hand,
one cannot deny that MacLennan is right to emphasise the
harmful effects of what he, one suspects, would call second-
hand tradition. It nourished, in the upper levels of English-
speaking society, the attitude which was partially responsible
for Janet Methuen's betrayal of Marius—an inhuman action
—and, generally speaking, a patronising discrimination toward
French Canadians by the denizens of Westmount and the
Town of Mount Royal.

If one were to choose a typical landscape description of
MacLennan's, the following would be as good as any:

> That afternoon it blew cold from the northeast, the wind
> built itself up, towards evening the air was flecked with a
> scud of white specks, and then the full weight of the snow
> began to drive. It whipped the land, greyed it, then turned it
> white and continued to come down hissing invisibly after
> dark all night long until mid-morning of the next day. For a
> few days after that the river was like black ink pouring
> between the flat whiteness of the plains on either side. Then
> the frost cracked down harder, the river stilled and froze.
> Another blizzard came and covered the ice, and then the
> whole world was so white you could hardly look at it with
> the naked eye against the glittering sun in the morning. The
> farmhouses seemed marooned. . . .[12]

MacLennan is not fond of figurative language—metaphors
and similes are few and far between in his writing. The
strength of this spare prose lies in its clarity; ordinary
language is used to convey the sense of something seen and
remembered. To the reader such pictures are real; if he is
familiar with Montreal or the Saint Lawrence Valley, say,
the impact is immediate, and he is liable to give the author
more credit than he deserves, artistically speaking. Familiarity negates, to some extent, the lack of an original or really

exciting prose style, but certainly straight-forward visual, often sensuous, description serves its purpose admirably.

One outstanding fault in the novel is a deliberate tilting of the story towards an American audience. "Since the confederation of the provinces into the Dominion of Canada just after the American Civil War, a Tallard had always sat in parliament in Ottawa." [13] This is far too explicit, and is a blatant concession to the American reader. If Americans don't know the date of Confederation or the location of Canada's parliament, let them look up the details elsewhere. A more flagrant and annoying instance reads: "A year ago Drouin had introduced another decoration for the store-front, a small bracket over the door holding three faded flags. One was the Red Ensign of the British Mercantile Marine with a Canadian crest in the corner." [14] A Canadian reader was bound to be indignant at the assumption that he did not know what his own flag looked like. It is as if an American writer were to describe his flag not as "the stars and stripes," but rather as "a design originated by Betsy Ross, who lived in Philadelphia. . . ." MacLennan's audience is, after all, predominantly Canadian—and most Canadians, one imagines, particularly if they are as concerned about nationalism as MacLennan is, will resent this clumsy bowing and scraping toward the south.

Except for this flaw, the banal bedroom scene, and the disturbing presence of Kathleen and Yardley, the first half of *Two Solitudes* is skilfully and convincingly written. One sees in microcosm, and begins to comprehend, a major problem that besets this country. More important, one arrives at this understanding through being involved in the tragic predicament of living characters. Here, in the first two hundred and twenty-five pages of *Two Solitudes*, MacLennan comes very close indeed to creating a "whole which is harmonious."

Nothing like as much can be said for the second half of the book. George Woodcock has written that

If *Two Solitudes* had ended with Tallard's death, it would have been a moving and cohesive book. But up to this point it merely presents the problem of racial relations; it does not have the logical completeness of presenting a solution, and this MacLennan seeks, at the expense of his novel, in its later chapters.[15]

—and he is right, as is Desmond Pacey, who calls the second half "much inferior."[16] In this part of the book, structure, plot, characterisation, theme, and style all collapse, and one finds it hard to understand how a man who had been writing at the top of his form up to now could be responsible for this turgid shambles.

We leap a gap of thirteen years, from Tallard's death to 1934. Heather, Janet's younger daughter, breaks away from the cloying restrictions of the elite society in which she has been brought up and falls in love with Paul. The two of them meet at Yardley's Montreal apartment—he has left Saint-Marc, which by now has long been a factory town. Paul has, since his father's death, travelled across Canada on various jobs and has played professional hockey to put himself through college; he has taken a degree and, with Kathleen remarried, is entirely on his own. He has intentions of becoming a novelist, and he and Heather are together for only a short time, for he wants "to see the world" and Part Three of the novel, 1934, ends with him outward bound from Halifax Harbour.

Five years flash by and we find ourselves in 1939, the final quarter of the book. Paul has, in the interim, not only been a seaman; he has sold short stories to American magazines and, on the strength of his Canadian degree, has gone to Oxford. (His college, like MacLennan's, was Oriel.) There he began work on a novel and he has come to Greece to finish it. Unable to, however, and homesick, he has planned his return to Canada.

Back home, Yardley has returned to Nova Scotia. He lives in a lodging house in Halifax where Janet and Heather have been visiting him. Janet is worried about Heather's having discarded her proper social circle (She has been studying art in New York.) and also about her lasting infatuation for Paul. Yardley, having rebuked his daughter for her attitude, dies. The scene dealing with his death is easily the best in the second half of the book. Paul has come back, and he and

Heather are secretly married in Halifax. Three unmemorable chapters are given to their honeymoon trip to Montreal via the Gaspé. In Montreal, Paul refuses to concede to Janet's wishes for him, and gets down to work on a novel. He visits Marius, who lives with his wife and a slew of children in a grubby working-class neighbourhood; the older brother is an impoverished lawyer, and his bitter nationalistic idealism has become almost his sole purpose of existence.

As the novel moves to its close, Heather and her mother —who does not know of the marriage—are vacationing in Maine. McQueen, who has remained Janet's intimate advisor, is encouraged by her to persuade Heather to break with Paul. This forces Heather's hand, and her mother, when she learns the truth, feigns a serious attack. As this is going on, the war begins, and Paul, who is to enlist the following day, arrives to join his wife. Heather has at last made a clean break with her mother and all that she stands for; but reconciliation on Janet's part is implied at the end.

The plot of the novel finishes there. But then comes an incredibly poor, if brief, concluding chapter. We are given a quick cross-country tour of Canada, we read of its preparations for war, and, finally, we are subjected to this fuzzy piece of pontifical philosophising:

> Then, even as the two race-legends woke again remembering ancient enmities, there woke with them also the felt knowledge that together they had fought and survived one great war they had never made and that now they had entered another; that for nearly a hundred years the nation had been spread out on the top half of the continent over the powerhouse of the United States and still was there; that even if the legends were like oil and alcohol in the same bottle, the bottle had not been broken yet. And almost grudgingly, out of the instinct to what was necessary, the country took the first irrevocable steps toward becoming herself, knowing against her will that she was not unique but like all the others, alone with history, with science, with the future.[17]

This paragraph is, regrettably, an almost inevitable conclusion; for MacLennan, in the second half of *Two Solitudes,* is primarily interested in proselytizing. The plot and the characters are subjected to the theme, and as a result the theme degenerates into a tiresome lecture.

A plot is sustained by the actions of its characters, actions which must, in a realistic novel, develop from convincing emotions and beliefs, which in their turn must stem from believable, living, personalities. The two protagonists here, Paul and Heather, are, artistically speaking, failures. Paul is meant to symbolise, through his union with Heather, the desired harmony of French-with English-speaking Canada. But he is just as unreal as his mother. One never really learns why he has developed into the person he is—only that he had a tough time in the depression, that he went to sea and to Oxford, etc. Rather than take the time to illuminate Paul's character in Part Three, MacLennan hurriedly jumps to Part Four, anxious, seemingly, to deliver his message. Our discomfort with Paul is generated in large part by this emptiness of understanding. He steps into the second half of the book a ready-made hero. He does too many things which, taken together, have a "romantic" aura about them: labourer to hockey-star to sailor to Oxford man to novelist. Indeed, by the time he gets to Greece—just twenty-nine—his hair is, in the best women's-magazine tradition, "foxed with grey."

It is apparent that Paul is mainly a projection of the author himself—not entirely an autobiographical figure, but certainly one whose activities bear a striking resemblance to MacLennan's. This is borne out not only by Paul's time at Oriel and in Greece, but, more obviously, through his ideas on the novel. There is no good reason for his being a novelist, and one can only suppose that this was done so as to give the author a chance to air, and defend, his own views on writing about Canada. One sees that Paul's developing attitude is the same as was MacLennan's:

In every city the same masses swarmed. Could any man write a novel about masses? The young man of 1933, together with all the individuals Paul had tried to create, grew pallid and unreal in his imagination beside the sense of the swarming masses heard three stories below in the shuffling feet of the crowd. For long minutes he stood at the window. To make a novel out of this? How could he? How could anyone? A novel should concern people, not ideas, and yet people had become trivial.[18]

This refers to that novel MacLennan tried to write before the war—the one with "an international setting." By the time Paul goes on his honeymoon, his artistic philosophy is carried to the conclusion that, as we have seen earlier, Mac-Lennan himself reached. Heather (Dorothy Duncan?) has read Paul's now-finished book. Her criticism leads him to exclaim,

"Maybe I shouldn't have chosen a European scene. Of course, Europe is the focus . . ." He jumped up and began walking back and forth. "My God!" he shouted, "I've been a fool! A year's work! Heather—I've wasted a year's work!"
She looked at him in excitement. Her thoughts were on the same track as his own. "Paul, why didn't you set the scene in Canada?"

Paul follows this up with the following argument:

Must he write out of his own background, even if that background were Canada? Canada was imitative in everything. Yes, but perhaps only on the surface. What about underneath? No one had dug underneath so far, that was the trouble. . . . Canada was a country no one knew. . . . There was the question of background. As Paul considered the matter, he realised that his readers' ignorance of the essential Canadian clashes and values presented him with a unique problem. The background would have to be created from scratch if his story was to become intelligible. He could afford to take nothing for granted. He would have to build the stage and props for his play, and then write the play itself.[19]

Two Solitudes preceded MacLennan's first volume of essays, *Cross Country,* the contents of which were all written after the novel was published. So this passage is his first declaration in print of what he has set out to do, and why he is following the pattern that he does; in that respect it is both interesting and informative. But, seen in its entirety, this passage does not read much like a thought process and, unfortunately, could be taken as a justification, or defence, of the methods employed in writing *Barometer Rising* (a belated reply to critics?) or *Two Solitudes.* "A novel should concern people, not ideas, and yet people had become trivial," thought Paul. Here we see ideas taking over, and Paul's own reality is diminished.

MacLennan tends to fall back on a style which wrecked *Barometer Rising,* but which had all but disappeared in the first half of *Two Solitudes.* Stilted philosophising takes the place of internal revelation. Here is Paul as he works on his new novel:

> Out of the society which had produced and frustrated him, which in his own way he had learned to accept, he knew that he was at last beating out a harmony. . . . In all his life, he had never seen an English-Canadian and a French-Canadian hostile to each other face to face. When they disliked, they disliked entirely in the group. And the result of these two group-legends was a Canada oddly naive, so far without any real villains, without overt cruelty or criminal memories, a country strangely innocent in its groping individual common sense, intent on doing the right thing in the way some children are, tongue-tied because it felt others would not be interested in what it had to say; loyal, skilled and proud, race-memories lonely in great spaces.[20]

If one assigns these ideas to MacLennan as well—and one must—there is a discrepancy, petty though it may seem; in this novel we have seen English- and French-Canadians "'hostile to each other face to face;" McQueen and Tallard, Marius and the soldier who accosted him, and, shortly now, Janet and Paul. Paul, then, is emasculated by the author's style; he is like Neil MacRae—a humourless hollow man, and too obviously an unreal symbolic figure for us to identify with him.

Heather has no real impact. She acts as a foil for Paul's usually turgid polemics and is in all respects an extremely commonplace heroine; like Penelope Wain, she is mature, intelligent, attractive, and strong-willed but loyal to Paul. She is used mainly as a commentator on the faults of Montreal high society, and is a representative of new tolerance and harmony between the English and French. Also, she is employed—as was Penny—as a weapon against Canadian restrictions on women who desire a career of their own.

As protagonists, both Paul and Heather fail because they never capture our imagination or admiration. The ideas they extol are interesting enough, but, as in *Barometer Rising,* these ideas lose their attraction because one is always conscious that one is reading a work of fiction—the frequent interruptions while dreary characters deliver lectures diminish our interest; MacLennan, as a craftsman, never makes up his mind whether to fish (write fiction) or cut bait (write non-fiction), and this indecisiveness is all too apparent to the reader.

The other four major characters are more successful. McQueen retains his pompous stupidity and Janet her neurotic unpleasantness. The two of them, along with Daphne, Heather's older sister, enable MacLennan to continue in this half of the book his sarcastic satire of their background. These three, and other peripheral figures, live in the pages because they speak far more than they think, and MacLennan's handling of dialogue—he has a good ear for regional accents and idiom—is crisply competent. Yardley sagaciously admonishes us and the characters until he dies, but he is more believable now that he is out of Saint-Marc. His reminiscences of his years at sea as he lies dying appeal to our emotions and imagination more than anything else in this half of the novel; these memories are vivid and have a sensory quality that typifies MacLennan's writing at its best. And then, this:

It was strange how a man's life passed like a ship through different kinds of weather. . . . Wonder in childhood; in the twenties physical violence and pride in muscles; in the thirties ambition; in the forties caution, and maybe a lot of dirty work; and then, if you were lucky, perhaps you could grow mellow. It seemed to Yardley that with the talent and the courage there was no limit to what a man could obtain out of life if he merely accepted what lay all around him. But knowledge was necessary; otherwise beauty was wasted. Beauty had come to him late in life, but now he couldn't have enough of it. It was something a man had to understand. Pictures and colours, for instance, and fine glass.[21]

This thematic undertone which we first noticed in *Barometer Rising* with Angus Murray—of thankfulness for the wonder of life—we will next see, in greatly expanded form, in *The Watch That Ends the Night.*

These characters, however, do not play a large enough part to rescue the second-half plot from the protagonists. Other debilitating factors—closely related, as we have seen, to the failure of Paul and Heather—are the crippling structure, the dead weight of thematic context, and an almost incomprehensible falling-off of technique. The structure is arranged, first of all so as to bring a mature Paul and Heather together, and secondly to bring them to the brink of the Hitler War, which, it is suggested in that disastrous concluding chapter, will forge a new national unity. The theme controls the structure and the characters, both of which aspects wreck the plot.

The first half of *Two Solitudes* is one of MacLennan's most disciplined and coherent efforts at craftsmanship. Clearly, however, he was artistically negligent in the second half of the book. Once one moves from 1921 to 1934 one finds oneself in a new story. The connexion between the halves is tenuous at best. The characters do, of course, provide a link, but one is concerned mainly with Paul's theorising and his affair with Heather. One misses the fiery Marius and Tallard's sad battle against overwhelming odds. Not only is unity of time and action lost, but also the unity of place, the intricate and meaningful contrast between Saint-Marc and Montreal. From a tightly knit, intelligently written, and believable tragedy we move into what is supposed to be a confident reconciliation—only to find it a boring, fragmentary denouement. With the death of Tallard, MacLennan's imagination failed him; falling back on his own experience and private philosophy he tried to keep the theme going; it did, but the novel stopped dead. Giving every credit to the first half of the book, one must in the last analysis condemn the author for starting a job and failing to finish it. The last one hundred and forty-one pages are a flimsy excuse for fiction; the halves of the novel are themselves solitudes.

CHAPTER FOUR

⌣ THE PRECIPICE

"The Precipice . . . *is of great interest to an 'American'*
reader."
Edmund Wilson[1]

". . . The Precipice *is an almost complete failure."*
Desmond Pacey[2]

". . . The Precipice, *MacLennan's worst novel."*
George Woodcock[3]

Perhaps my life has made this third book inevitable. Ever
since I returned to Canada I have been going back to the
United States each year. . . . No good can come from the
pretence that societies and nations do not differ from one
another. Many differences between Canadians and Americans
it will do us good to recognise.[4]

IN *The Precipice,* Hugh MacLennan chose a theme which
he felt to be just as important for Canada as that of *Two*
Solitudes. Determined to say something profound about the
relationship between Canada and the United States, he
examines, and contrasts, the values of the two countries; but
in doing so he neglects his craft and, ultimately, fails in his
aim. MacLennan seems to have forgotten that the reader
of serious realistic novels wants, if he is to be instructed, to
be entertained at the same time: that is, one looks for all,
or at least one, of the following—appealing style, an interesting
plot, and moving, vivid characters. If these aspects are
wanting, the reader will, as he loses interest in the story,

cease to care about the theme as well; which is what happens in *The Precipice*. MacLennan, mainly through a failure of imagination, destroys his own purpose.

The trouble begins with the plot, a cliché in itself. What MacLennan has done is to fall back upon romance as a means of explicating his thesis. This in itself, as we will see, is the easy way out, but, what is worse, the romance is one with which we were all too familiar before we opened the book: briefly, a girl from a small country town and a man from a city fall in love; they each illustrate the virtues and shortcomings of their environments and, after experiencing some well-worn pitfalls of courtship and marriage, they live (one is led to suppose) happily ever after.

Grenville, a small town on the Lake Ontario shore where "Canada breathed out the last moments of her long Victorian sleep," is the setting for the first half of the novel.

> Grenville was . . . a town of eight thousand people who had been stiff-necked from the day the first United Empire Loyalist had marked out his lot a century and a half ago, constantly right in its judgements but usually for the wrong reasons. Here was lodged the hard core of Canadian matter-of-factness on which men of imagination had been breaking themselves for years. Grenville was sound, it was dull, it was loyal, it was competent—and oh, God, it was so Canadian! The ferments and the revolutions of the past twenty years might never have existed so far as this town was concerned. Until the Grenvilles of Canada were debunked from top to bottom . . . there would be no fun and no future for anyone in the country.[5]

Immediately the book begins, we find a preponderance of such dogmatic commentary; MacLennan dives headlong into his theme with a complete lack of subtlety and loses no time in telling us what the novel is going to be about. Dullness and lack of initiative—stemming from an inherent puritanical conservatism—are clearly under attack.

It is here that Stephen Lassiter, the hero, meets and woos Lucy Cameron, the heroine. Lassiter, ruggedly handsome, is an "efficiency-expert" who has been sent to Grenville to straighten out problems in the town's only factory, which is American-controlled. Lucy, age twenty-seven, is one of three sisters who live together in the house of their dead parents. She is attractive in a very wholesome fashion, is intelligent and quiet, and is aware of the stagnant aspects of existence in Grenville. Throughout most of the novel she is at odds with her older sister, Jane, a narrow-minded, reactionary spinster who resents Lucy's love for Lassiter. Nina, the youngest of the trio, a light-headed, petulant flirt, rebels much more vehemently against Grenville than does Lucy. Each of the three represents a different attitude toward the town— and life generally—and their continuing conflict is one of the few semi-interesting segments of the story.

The romance gets heavily under way when Lucy, upon seeing Lassiter for the first time, thinks "if this man is important, then everyone else I know is not." Such stiff, trite clichés smack of *The Ladies' Home Journal* or of a third-rate Hollywood production, and typify their whole affair. One knows instinctively at this point that they are going to fall in love and that Stephen will take Lucy away to the big city. MacLennan's treatment of their developing relationship is most awkward: "By accepting her as a woman he showed her she was like other women after all, and like them desirable. Her world staggered and moved, but she moved with it. After that August night in Grenville, Lucy never felt herself a spectator again." [6] Lassiter falls in love with her because she seems to represent a simpler, better world than the one he is accustomed to:

"I was thinking of you in the garden. It shows on your face, what you feel about that garden. You're beautiful in a way hardly any women are any more. The women you see in New York crossing the Plaza at five o'clock are supposed to be the most wonderful in the world, but they don't look like you. They never remind anybody of a garden." [7]

Lucy (or is it Doris Day?) reminds him not only of flowers, but also of his mother: "I remembered the way you'd looked at trees and flowers as if nobody had ever seen them before. Nobody has looked at me the way you do since I was a kid." [8]

This boring dalliance is regularly punctuated by thematic interludes in which MacLennan tries to point up those "differences it will do us good to recognise." The protagonists have to batter their sentimental way into each other's arms through thickets of this material.

"This whole town's got ability. There's a real quality about it. But you all think too small. You could never be dangerous. You see a small town in the United States, in the South or the Middle West I mean, and the people are crude compared to you people here. But they can be dangerous. You can never be sure what they might do." [9]

(One notices what we will see to be one of the most ruinous flaws in the book in this passage; it is implied—inadvertently, perhaps—that towns in, say, New England are a lot like Grenville; and nothing is said about towns in Manitoba or Alberta—are the Canadians who live out there "crude" and "dangerous?" MacLennan is silent on this point.) Thus, even while we are told that Lucy is attracted by Lassiter's loneliness rather than by the sort of life he stands for, we are constantly aware of the fact that MacLennan is not truly interested in his characters as human beings; instead, we know that an antique and shallow plot is almost entirely the vehicle for his didactic intent.

A certain degree of verisimilitude is given to the story by two lesser figures, Matt McCunn, Lucy's iconoclastic uncle, and Carl Bratian, a friend of Lassiter's who is driven solely by "an authentic money-hunger." McCunn encourages Lucy to marry Lassiter, and Bratian, cold and hard, shows how Lassiter may end up if Lucy doesn't save him. Stephen, it turns out, is already married, but has been separated and is getting a divorce; this lends momentary turbulence to the sluggish story, as Lucy holds off marrying him—but in the end, of course, she does.

It is unfortunate that the plot is further paralysed when MacLennan, as the omniscient author, chooses to deliver a history lesson:

During that September in Canada, as everywhere else in the western world, people shared the same agony of fear and shame when Hitler revealed that he was at last in a position to disgrace the entire human race. When Chamberlain went to Munich something happened in Canada which few people understood at the time. Outside of Quebec, they had been taught from childhood to believe that their principal glory as a people rested on the fact that they were part of the British Empire. But along with this sense of continuance from the Old Country, which Americans had largely lost through the revolution, they had for years accepted British foreign policy like a handed-down suit of clothes. Now a psychological break occurred. Inarticulate people began to realise that Canada, in fact, was standing more and more alone. . . . Unlike the Americans, they knew they would be in it from the beginning, and it gave them a feeling of being trapped.[10]

This passage is noteworthy for several reasons. First, in spite of the accurate interpretation of history which it contains, it is stylistically crippling, is not conducive to the flow of the fictional narrative. Secondly, there *are* historical implications here which, if examined, would go a long way toward explaining major differences between Canadians and Americans. Aside from a few hints such as we find here, MacLennan never explores the impact of history upon his theme—with the result that the theme, as we will notice, becomes too thin and brittle to support the space given it. Lastly, the tone of the passage, and the wording ("they had been taught . . .") suggests very strongly that it is directed to the American reader—the same weakness one saw in *Two Solitudes*.

Part One, the first half of the book, closes with Lucy and Stephen, just married, in New York:

The weight of her head against his shoulder finally woke Stephen. He stirred and she heard him murmur her name; then he surged up, a shadowy mass against the pale frame of the window, his arms came about her again, and with a slow and formidable tenderness he held her close. Out of the darkness she heard her own voice calling his name.[11]

This stale paragraph reflects all too well the plot itself, and bodes ill for the second half of the book.

Part Two, which occurs more than a year later, is very short—thirty-three pages. In it, we learn that Lassiter and Lucy, despite business pressures (he has taken a job with Bratian in advertising) are happily married. Bruce Fraser is the temporary protagonist here; he is a neighbour of Lucy's from Grenville, now in the R.C.A.F., who has come to visit the Lassiters and to see New York. Through him, one is introduced to the excitement of Manhattan, and most of the accompanying description is competently evocative. However, as is so often the case, MacLennan's sense of proportion fails him; he is guilty of treating one simple occurrence with an embarrassing grandiloquence—Bruce is having his shoes done by an itinerant Italian shoe-shiner:

> Once or twice he looked up at the man above him, the yellowish whites of his eyes showing, but he had no way of guessing what lay in Bruce's mind. Perhaps he wondered if this tense young foreigner would some day drop bombs on the helpless little town in Southern Italy which he had left years ago to follow a dream of making a great success in America. Perhaps he thought only of the difference which stood between them, the one blue-eyed, keen and erect, quick and dangerous, the kind of man invariably chosen to drop bombs; the other on his knees, loose and shapeless, yet slow and softly durable, with inarticulate, useless but ultimate knowledge in his eyes.[12]

Bruce, a virgin, symbolises in a flimsy sort of way Canada's "innocence" and her straightforward brand of responsibility and courage. Stephen and Lucy introduce him to Stephen's sister, Marcia, a highly sophisticated but disillusioned siren, who finds him appealing because of his "cleanness" and old-fashioned simplicity. (Would a boy from Minnesota or Maine be much different?) She seduces him (although by now he realises he loves Lucy) and after contemplating this momentous event in MacLennan's most ambitious use of metaphor in the novel (". . . he was not sure whether he had crossed the frontier of a deeper mystery or merely entered the first of a long series of rooms") his leave ends, and he goes off to the war. This part of the plot is too much a fragment to carry its weight; Bruce, who is transparently being manipulated for thematic purposes and who, anyway, is a dull, self-pitying character from beginning to end, is in a spotlight that illuminates his weaknesses all too clearly. And descriptions of Manhattan, unless exceptionally well-done (one thinks of Salinger or Thomas Wolfe) tend to echo one another. MacLennan is not Wolfe or Salinger.

Part Three is equally brief, and serves merely as a structural prop. It tells us what happens between 1940 and 1945 to the main figures in the novel. Bruce speaks about Canadian "self-knowledge" rising from wartime participation, and Nina, now a Wren, gives the author a chance to sketch Halifax for us. Bratian starts his own advertising agency and Lassiter works for him; MacLennan was the first novelist, to the best of this writer's knowledge, to examine the advertising game in any detail, and his satiric observations are well-founded. Lucy begins to resent Bratian, but she responds happily (we are told) to Stephen's "natural sexual gusto." There are intimations of disaster, however, as Stephen begins to drink heavily. From what happens after this—that is, in the remainder of the novel—one realises that these five years were decisive ones insofar as the relationship between Lassiter and Lucy is concerned. But MacLennan's interest in human experience is subjugated to the hobby- horse he is riding in *The Precipice,* and the delicate balance of the protagonists' personal conflict and love is ignored in order that we can be brought back to the topic under discussion.

Part Four underlines the futility of MacLennan's plot. Stephen, torn between love for his wife and subordination to Bratian, and infuriated by the absurdities of advertising, takes a mistress. Lucy grows homesick for Grenville: she "began to wonder if one of the causes of her failure to hold Stephen's love might not simply be the fact that he was an American and she was not." [13] The point is, that one never believes that the rift between them has anything to do with nationality; any woman, no matter where she came from, would be likely to break with Stephen as he drinks, whores, and ignores his family. This realisation detracts from the incessant emphasis upon Lucy's being a Canadian—one can usually understand her viewpoint where the United States is concerned, but one feels strongly that MacLennan is overdoing this aspect of the story.

As the 1939-45 War ends, Lucy listens to the radio:

A senator gave a patriotic address, a band played martial

music, and in all the time they listened nobody mentioned the name of Canada.

"We always win, don't we, Mummy?" John said. Lucy was startled by the significance of the pronoun, and her answering smile was for herself. Of course. Americans always won, and of course John was an American.[14]

Spurred by patriotic emotion as much as by the apparent ruin of her marriage, Lucy takes the children and motors back to Grenville; she has been away for seven years.

Bruce has also returned, and his conversations with Lucy are used mainly to state nationalistic sentiments such as the following:

"It's going to be better all over Canada after the war . . . When the San Francisco Conference was over I went up the coast to Vancouver and came back on the Transcontinental. God, what a land to live in! When the train was crawling up that colossal grade under Cathedral Mountain an American in the observation car said to anyone who would listen to him, 'How the hell did Canadians manage to break a country like this without anybody shooting his mouth off about it?' . . . We're just beginning to discover ourselves. Americans had that excitement fifty to a hundred years ago. Ours is beginning now." [15]

Finally, Lucy learns that Stephen has been fired by Bratian and is in a Chicago hotel. She tells Bruce, who has been trying to win her over:

"The other night after we heard about the atomic bomb I began to think of Americans the way you do—like a great mass of people and not as individuals. I saw them moving in a vast swarm over a plain. They had gone faster and farther than any people had ever gone before. Each day for years they measured out the distance they'd advanced. They were trained to believe there was nothing any of them could do but keep on travelling in the same way. And then suddenly they were brought up short at the edge of a precipice which hadn't been marked on the map. There they were with all their vehicles and equipment, jostling and piling up on the front rank. . . . And there was Stephen himself, heaving and pushing without realising the significance of what he was doing, in a rank not very far from the front." [16]

This vision (the implications of which are discussed below) and a concomitant desertion-complex cause Lucy to return to the man she loves. In a reconciliation scene reminiscent of some of Hollywood's poorer technicolor features, they apologise to one another, and MacLennan's histrionic sentimentality runs amuck:

Stephen had reached the end of the same road Marcia had taken, had followed to the same source most of the marsh-lights which had appeared to his generation like rising suns. . . . Now he had reached the yawning edge of the precipice and he knew it was there, he knew the map he had followed was no longer of any use.[17]

To atone for his guilt, Lassiter informs his wife that he is going away to drive a truck in northern Minnesota. But as the sun sets on this atrocious finale we know from the last sentences that all is going to be alright: "It's the beginning, she thought. Once again, it's a beginning." At last, we, too, reach the yawning edge of *The Precipice*.

In outline, then, the plot is seen to be not only hackneyed, but overly and awkwardly involved, structurally weak, shot through with unassimilated passages, and glutted with thematic detail; MacLennan's preface to the novel is theatrical and enigmatic and the ending strikes a similarly hollow note.

By examining the characters it will be possible to see more clearly where the author draws the line between Americans and Canadians. Stephen's life is, essentially, the proverbial American Success Story gone sour. His father was that stock-character, the American who has risen from a poor boyhood ("a dirt farm forty miles west of St. Louis") to wealth. Not too surprisingly, he thought his children had it soft compared to him:

Stephen had never forgotten a book his father had given him once for his birthday. It was called *Great Men of America,* and apart from Thomas Edison, there was not a man in the book who was not an industrialist, a financier, or a railroad king. Their lives had seemed to Stephen depressingly similar. Each had his own variation of the same formula for success. Each had his own variation of the same look in the eyes. "Outside of Morgan," Abel Lassiter told his son, "there was hardly one of them who had it soft the way you do." [18]

As if that were not enough, just to keep Abel a folk-figure, MacLennan says that he was the sort who almost always gave his children money on birthdays and Christmas instead of the presents which would indicate true love. Such a fellow may be tiresome, but his story becomes semi-ludicrous when we learn that he, an uneducated fanatic, married into the New England aristocracy; MacLennan's explanation is that "frail women like powerful men." However, there is method in the author's madness, for this connubial fantasy helps to emphasise an aspect of the theme; Stephen says at one point to Lucy that the women of his mother's family "want to turn the whole United States into one goddam big museum." Translated, this means that his mother's people stand for roots and tradition—in much the same way that Jane does. Old Abel knew better, and he justified the many moves he forced his family to make: "A year or two more in the country and I'd have been putting down roots," he said. "If you want to get ahead, don't buy a house. Your family will get to like it and raise hell when you want to move on." Such men as Abel Lassiter do exist. But we have met him too often before, and as a result we are unable to accept his impact on his son as readily as perhaps we should: "Ever since he could remember, Stephen had been haunted by the feeling that he could never measure up to the men his father had tamed and mastered." [89]

But this guilt, for MacLennan, is much more the result of nationality than of blood and upbringing. Marcia explains her own and her brother's predicament:

". . . the puritans made us *live* with our guilt. They shamed us with our own humanity. For three hundred years we've lived on this continent in that same puritan tradition without ever knowing ourselves forgiven, and that's why we've become so callous and hard and rebellious. Even when we no longer believe in the God of our ancestors, the old guilt-habit stays. That's the trouble with Steve and I know it's the trouble with me—trying to run away from ourselves, not by finding something better but just trying to escape. Three hundred years of unspent pleasures in the bank, and every one of us thinking we had the combination of the vault." [20]

There is no doubt whatsoever that this interpretation is MacLennan's, for he has written elsewhere:

America's crisis, and therefore the crisis of the rest of us, consists in this; puritanism has conditioned its members to act rather than think, to deal with means rather than ends, to press forward with ever-increasing speed and efficiency toward a material goal. Today, after having advanced further into a materialistic paradise than any other people, Americans find themselves staring over the edge of a precipice, unable to make up their minds where to go. [21]

The essay from which this is drawn was written in January 1948—MacLennan must just have been finishing *The Precipice.*

Where the problem comes in is that the author attributes Stephen's mad rush for the precipice of materialism almost solely to the puritan ethic. Certainly this has been a shaping force in the development of the American temperament; but equally important is the American Revolution itself, and subsequent history. With the rebellion, stability of tradition was thrust aside and then the west began to open up; any man had his chance to make a fortune if he could—the principles of democracy inspire as much guilt in a man as does a puritan background; "I am equal to him—we have the same opportunity. I should do as well, or better; if I don't, there's something wrong with me." MacLennan's explanation of Stephen's guilt and money-lust is too one-sided, and too baldly stated at that, to be convincing.

Lassister also represents his country in his looks:

This was a face millions of people would recognise even if they didn't know the man himself. It was authentic American; a product of what the United States so often does to the original Anglo-Saxon mould. It was larger and bolder than the faces of most Canadian men she knew, but somehow its lines were less decisive . . . The eyes looked boyish. The mouth, when he concentrated, looked hard. When he grinned he was very attractive. It was the face of a man who expects most people to like him exactly as he is. [22]

And: "Remembering Lassiter's tanned face, she noticed how the English and Scottish ruddiness predominated in the complexions of all these Grenville men." [23] It is hard to know how to respond to MacLennan's opinion on physiognomy. He may well be correct in suggesting that an American can be recognised at a glance. But (to be contentious) would it really be all that easy to tell the St. James Street broker from his Wall Street cousin, or a North Dakota farmer from a farmer who comes from Manitoba?

In the first half of the novel Lassiter is believable in spite of his unnatural mumblings of love to Lucy. However, he is a stereotype with whom one is all too familiar—the big, tough American, good in bed, out for all he can get, and riding for a fall. When we move to the second half of the book, Bratian comes more and more alive and steals Stephen's fire just as Murray did MacRae's. We are supposed to recognise a definite goodness in Stephen as compared to Bratian, but this sensibility is never evinced. To bear out the motive behind the novel, and to give Lassiter at least some last-minute stature, he should break away from Bratian and the advertising business instead of drinking himself out of a job. But by the time one sees the last of Lassiter one simply thinks of him as an unsuccessful, self-pitying Bratian —this, regardless of his technicolor propitiation at the end.

Carl Bratian is an up-to-date version of Stephen's father. He comes of poor immigrant parents, is intelligent, and uses the conventions of American life to his own advantage. He utilises not only custom, but people as well; to him, the only important aim in life is success in terms of wealth. More clever than Stephen, he is also given a much more forceful dialogue—cynically realistic, with pervasive sinister undertones. One can appreciate Lucy's distaste for, and fear of him, for he lures Stephen into a business built largely upon deceit and self-degradation. As a "free agent" in the novel, he is not shackled to the platitudinous atmosphere that envelops Stephen's union with Lucy; although his type is not uncommon in fiction, he is a rounded character who, despite his money-hunger, has considerable insight into other people and an appreciation of values other than his own. One believes in him enough to both despise and pity him—as the author intended.

The author intended as well that we admire Lucy, but she shares that lifelessness that is a trademark of nearly all MacLennan heroines. We have seen that her characteristics are similar to those of Penny Wain and Heather Methuen. And she follows the formula further, by breaking away from the old order in which she's been brought up. Throughout the book one is told over and over again by nearly all the leading figures— Stephen, Bratian, McCunn, Marcia, Bruce—that Lucy has superb qualities; unfortunately, the reader is at a loss to know what they are. One knows that she did well in university, keeps a flower garden, likes to read, and loves Stephen, but one cannot accept MacLennan's oblique insistence on her thoroughbred nature. This fuzziness of Lucy is primarily caused by her continuing harping, in thought and speech, on the theme; secondly, of course, she is the victim of a trite plot and concomitant sentimental distortion. Occasionally she comes alive when quarrelling with Jane and Nina or with Bratian. But even here one is not interested in her dilemma for there is nothing about her to excite our admiration.

Just as Bratian's vitality causes Lassiter to shrink in our mind's eye, Lucy is dwarfed in her encounters with the most enjoyable and genuine character in the novel, her Uncle Matt McCunn. An unfrocked minister of adventurous background, he is iconoclastic, fond of the bottle, and is the local ne'er-do-well. Whenever he appears he creates a refreshing interlude, the only realised modulation in the book. For instance, Lucy is telling him of her love for Stephen: "Why," he asks, "don't you get in bed with the big bastard?" (It is a telling commentary on the tedium of the novel that such a remark is a high point.) He also tells Lucy that much goes on in Grenville that she's not aware of: "They're a lusty lot here. . . . Don't judge them by Jane and your father. Those two just happen to be the incarnate images of the kind of morality the rest of them pretend to believe in but really don't." [24] MacLennan was wise to bring this in, for no small town is entirely dull; each is stratified, and most tend to be as much like John Cheever's St. Botolph's[25] as they are like the part of the

Grenville iceberg that shows above water. Like Murray and
Yardley, McCunn is well-read and is given to delivering
thematic profundities. But he is much more a goatish adven-
turer than a wise old man, and his colourful comments are an
oasis in this desert of a book.

Jane Cameron, the antithesis of McCunn, is also a flesh
and blood figure. A mixture of Aunt Maria Wain and Janet
Methuen, she is a domineering ultra-conservative, and typifies
(for MacLennan) the worst aspects of a "Grenville" upbringing. An avid champion of things English, she is also anti-
American; here she is telling Lucy she ought to write a book

". . . about the Loyalists. . . . You could write about our
ancestor who was a judge in Massachusetts before they
burned his house down and nearly murdered him. The
Americans admire themselves so much, it would be a good
thing if somebody reminded them about the other side of
their picture. They've become intolerably conceited and it
would do them good if someone took them down a peg or
two."[26]

Such straightforward opinions provide a welcome respite
from Lucy's dragged-out agonising. But Jane does not entirely
work as a symbol of Canadian "retrogression" (something
which has its appealing side, anyway). She could just as
easily be a woman from any small town in the United States
—a Georgian commenting on the Yankees, say. Again, it
speaks ill for the novel when as hackneyed a figure of fiction
as Jane is one of the few characters who captures our interest.

Nina, the youngest sister, an empty-headed man hunter,
plays a very minor part. Aside from acting as a sounding-
board between her sisters, she is used chiefly as a denigrator
of Grenville. Like all the other characters, she is made to
shoulder a portion of the theme: "Another vague formula
which Nina shared in common with many Canadians told
her that she was somewhat superior to Americans, though
she never asked herself why, or expected Americans to recognise the superiority."[27] This would be a worth-while line to
follow up, but MacLennan never does.

Bruce Fraser's function in *The Precipice* is to represent
both Canadian "innocence" and the frustrated potential of

Canadian youth. He is required to talk about Canada or the United States at frequent intervals, thus adding to the topical catalogue; his most important comments are upon the new spirit of Canadian identity that results from participation in the war. Bruce, however, is stillborn when we first meet him and he remains that way.

Bruce's seductress, Marcia, is a sociologist masquerading as a playgirl. Her role in the book, like his, is to contribute intermittent manifestoes dealing with the theme. It is she who explains Stephen's plight in terms of a puritan heritage; but she also expounds upon a favourite obsession of MacLennan's :

I call us the well-meaning generation. We threw away the wisdom of the ages because we quite correctly despised our parents. In our own way we were so terribly moral. We slept with each other whenever we felt like it because we thought it was hypocritical not to follow our natural instincts. We believed that wars were made by munitions-makers and old men who should have been dead, and so we let this one become possible because we weren't going to let ourselves be fooled a second time. We thought science had arrived to take the place of religion, and we believed the only thing needed to make us good was a good economic system. Because our parents were wrong about nearly everything, we took it for granted we were automatically right whenever we disagreed with them. If Jesus Christ appeared to-day, we'd send him to a psychoanalyst to get rid of his maladjustments."[28]

Directly following this, we read: "Only a little of what Marcia said touched an emotional chord in Bruce, for he had met nobody in Canada who thought as she did, nor did her words agree with most American opinions he had seen in print." The point is that the words may be attributed to MacLennan. There is no doubt that he entertains a strong sense of association with, and great feeling of guilt for, his own generation. One can compare what Marcia says with the following excerpts from MacLennan's essay, "A Salutary Experience:"

My generation expected various ghastly ends, but we never took T.S. Eliot seriously when he said that the end of the

world (our world) would come not with a bang but a
whimper. . . . We were the ones who had known the score.
We had revolted against the stupidities of the old men,
against the Hoovers, the Baldwins, the Chamberlains and
the Hoare-Lavals. We had stood four-square for sexual eman-
cipation and the repeal of the Volstead Act and all its local
limitations. We had been for social reform and rationally
planned economies. . . . When Hemingway rediscovered
John Donne and asked for whom the bell tolls, we had
throbbed in unison with the answer that it tolled for us.[29]

MacLennan is not content to be spokesman for his country,
he must himself be the psychoanalyst of "his generation" as
well. We will see this masochistic lament developed at much
greater length in *The Watch That Ends the Night*.

The debilitating factor where the characters of *The Precipice* are concerned is that MacLennan does not care about
them as human beings. He is not really interested in how
these people react to one another—instead, he is intent upon
manipulating their emotions and thoughts to fit his pre-
conceived moralistic and sociological notions. Hence, most of
these characters become puppets, mouthpieces for the frown-
ing author behind the scenes; far too frequently we hear him
prompting them.

Since characterisation is weak, it might at least be expected
that the ideas which they represent are vital. Even here,
however, MacLennan has only partial success. Probably his
most discerning analysis in the novel is of Grenville. In many
ways it is an ordinary small-time North American community,
and it is convincingly shown as such. Where MacLennan
excels is in his interpretation of the effect of a puritanical
people upon this, their environment. For instance: ". . . the
Scotch and the Scotch-Irish who had flooded into Ontario
in the wake of the original Loyalist settlers had toughened
up everything they touched. It would be another hundred
years before any part of English-speaking Canada could hope
to be rid of what they had done to it."[30] Coupled with this
antagonism toward beauty, MacLennan points out, is a
Calvinistic dread of emotion, and these characteristics are
explained through a glance at the Cameron girls' dead father,
a Presbyterian minister. MacLennan's analysis of such towns

is affirmed in John Kenneth Galbraith's recent memoir of an Ontario boyhood, *The Scotch.*

However, useful as this analysis is, it only tends to obfuscate the over-all theme. On one side we have American puritanism which, we are assured, is the underlying cause of the maddened rush for the precipice south of the border. On the other side is Canadian puritanism—but this leads (it would seem) only to stagnation, to a weary dead-end. Where does the difference lie? MacLennan fails to explain this, in spite of the fact that each brand of puritanism is the basis of the national characteristic which he most deplores. Clearly, the answer must in part lie somewhere else—in race, in history, in geography; but these factors are virtually ignored. The result is that MacLennan's main thesis collapses and he is left with a number of valid, but unsatisfactorily elucidated, observations: Canadians are less boisterous than Americans, less assertive, less willing to take chances, more tied to tradition. The answers to these differences would have at least saved the novel from being as enigmatic as it is.

As was the case in the second half of *Two Solitudes, The Precipice* suffers badly from a lack of imagination, and this weakness extends, as has been noted, to theme, characterisation, structure, style and plot. Had MacLennan, let us say, moulded his plot around two men, one from Toronto, the other from New York, or one from Grenville, the other from Waterville, Maine, or Watertown, New York, he almost surely would have come up with a better novel. Grenville, after all, is not very different from any other small town, and Lucy could be any small-town girl; the derivative contrast between New York and Grenville, between slicker and wholesome flower-lover, as we have seen, only detracts from the author's aim—and would even if the theme had been handled brilliantly.

The relationship between two men (or women), each from a similar environment, would have been much more challenging, but far more rewarding as well. Then, perhaps, the more subtle and tantalising differences between the two countries could have been imaginatively contrasted and examined. One has only to think of a novel containing as protagonists Lassiter and Huntly McQueen; two men following the same star, not very different apparently—but going by MacLennan's own contention they must be. How? Why?

We have seen that all of MacLennan's first three novels are badly flawed. But this one lacks the dramatic excitement of *Barometer Rising* and the invigorating coherence of the first half of *Two Solitudes*—nor is it as good as the three books which follow it; there can be no doubt that *The Precipice* is Hugh MacLennan's least successful novel.

CHAPTER FIVE

⌒ EACH MAN'S SON

Scotland . . . received the Reformation without the Renais-
sance. The revival of the world of Greece brought to her not
beauty, not joy in life, but a sword and ill will to men. But
Scotland was not compelled, except by her own nature, to
accept the Reformation without the Renaissance. Calvinism
was not imposed on Scotland from without. It was accepted
because it was congenial to the national temperament.

R.L. Mackie[1]

It is Scottish Puritanism above everything else which is
responsible for an excessive sense of sin and guilt which has
alas! haunted so many good Scots folk for the last four
hundred years.

Moray McLaren[2]

The Highlanders of Scotland have suffered grievously from
oppression and enforced emigration in the last two centuries,
and there is an inescapable sadness in their race now which
once was not there.

Moray McLaren[3]

With them they brought—no doubt of this—that nameless
haunting guilt they never understood, and the feeling of
failure, and the loneliness . . .

Hugh MacLennan[4]

Eᴀᴄʜ Mᴀɴ's Sᴏɴ is Hugh MacLennan's best novel. The
reason for this is not very far to seek; MacLennan was writing
about himself, not his individual self, not his own life, but
rather about his ancestral consciousness, the spirit of his
inheritance. Thomas Wolfe, in *The Web and the Rock*, said
this:

In every man there are two hemispheres of light and dark;
two worlds discrete, two countries of his soul's adventure.
And one of these is the dark land, the other half of his
heart's home, the unvisited domain of his father's earth. . . .

MacLennan, in *Each Man's Son,* is visiting the dark domain.

We have seen elsewhere that his father was "a doctor who
spent much of his earlier life in a very hard practice in a
Cape Breton mining town." Although a third-generation
Canadian, "he never needed to go to the Highlands to understand whence he came or what he was."[5] And MacLennan
has said of himself that the knowledge of his heritage "seems
like a kind of doom from which I am too Scotch even to
think of praying for deliverance. I can thank my father for
this last-ditch neurosis."[6] His father was a descendant of
MacLennans who were driven from their own country and
who had added the burden of that guilt to their already
Calvinistic consciences. This is not to suggest that MacLennan
is writing about his father or that the novel is autobiographical. However, the book is autobiographical in spirit, for
MacLennan here uncovers emotions and beliefs that were
handed down to him by his forbears. MacLennan is not being
"romantic" when, in *Each Man's Son* he explores the guilt-
ridden conscience and scathing loneliness of Daniel Ainslie;
instead, he is being realistically empathetic, for he can
imagine himself in Ainslie's place, in an island whose people
and whose spirit he grew up with.

Yet, for all its merits, *Each Man's Son* is less well-known
than most of the other novels. The reason for this is at least
understandable. For the book is a *genre*-piece dealing with an
isolated environment and its people, who are, anyway,
notoriously misunderstood. Mention Highlanders, and people
think of jokes about the kilt, heather, castles—all the impe-
dimenta of a distorted romantic legend that owes its inception
to Walter Scott and Queen Victoria. If one is not a Highlander the only way to understand them is to understand
their history—particularly the Clearances. And if one person-
ally knows men of the Highlands, MacLennan's theme rings
all the truer; there is that sadness about them, that loneliness
that MacLennan saw in his own father—and it has not
disappeared:

... That harmony of folk and land is shattered,—
the yearly rhythm of things, the social graces,
peat-fire and music, candle-light and kindness.
Now they are gone it seems they never mattered,
much, to the world, those proud and violent races,
clansmen, and chiefs whose passioned greed and blindness
made desolate these lovely lonely places.

—the lines of a contemporary Scottish poet.[7]

If one hasn't an understanding of all this, one is liable to make the mistake Edmund Wilson does in evaluating *Each Man's Son:*

> Another book by Hugh MacLennan that does not seem to me successful is *Each Man's Son* (1951). Here one guesses that it must have occurred to him that he ought to do something about Calvinism, so depressing and hampering an influence on the mind of Presbyterian Canada, but one feels that the relationships and the mental crises which he contrives to illustrate this influence have, in the same way, not really been lived by the author.[8]

Wilson goes wrong for two reasons: first, MacLennan's previous didacticism, and recurrent mention of Calvinism, encourage such an attitude—if one does not understand MacLennan's relationship to Cape Breton and its people; second, Wilson has never been to Cape Breton. "I am told," he writes, "that there is even on the island of Cape Breton a kind of Cape Breton nationalism which makes a distinction between its own inhabitants and the rest of the population of Nova Scotia."[9] Seen in context, his tone is one of amused tolerance.

But, you might say, if a novel is any good, no matter what it is about, this should be apparent. George Woodcock, despite a rather fanciful interpretation built around the Odysseus legend, saw what MacLennan was doing:

> MacLennan himself comes from Cape Breton, and it is likely that the immediacy one feels in this novel, the tension that unites structure and theme and myth, and makes the characters convincingly human even when they are most the slaves of circumstances, stems from its closeness to his own experience.[10]

In fact, the theme—the repression of love through a combination of guilt and pride—and the action, a quest for compassion and personal fulfilment, are superbly unified.

MacLennan knew that only a handful of people would really comprehend what he had set out to do. To meet this problem, he would have to explain why the Highlanders came to Cape Breton, and what they were like; so, in order to lead his reader into the book without too great a handicap, he wrote an introduction doing just that. It is, up to a point, a fine introduction:

To Cape Breton the Highlanders brought more than the quixotic gallantry and softness of manner belonging to a Homeric people. They also brought with them an ancient curse, intensified by John Calvin and branded upon their souls by John Knox and his successors—the belief that man has inherited from Adam a nature so sinful there is no hope for him and that, furthermore, he lives and dies under the wrath of an arbitrary God who will forgive only a handful of His elect on the Day of Judgment.

As no normal human being can exist in constant awareness that he is sinful and doomed through no fault of his own, the Highlanders behaved outwardly as other men do who have softened the curse or forgotten its existence. But in Cape Breton they were lonely. They were no part of the great outer world. So the curse remained alive with them, like a somber beast growling behind an unlocked door. It was felt even when they were least conscious of it. To escape its cold breath some turned to drink and others to the pursuit of knowledge. . . . But they were still a fighting race with poetry in their hearts and a curse upon their souls. Each man's son was driven by the daemon of his own hope and imagination —by his energy or by his fear—to unknown destinations. For those who stayed behind, the beast continued to growl behind the unlocked door.[11]

The introduction should stop there; but, inexplicably, one comes to a nutshell analysis of Daniel Ainslie's character. As the book is primarily concerned with Ainslie, it is unfortunate that MacLennan gives his story away before he begins it—again, that carelessness about concern for the novel as an art form that we have by now become so aware of.

A major attribute of *Each Man's Son* it its compactness

and its concomitant sense of immediacy. There is none of
the sprawling disjointedness of *Two Solitudes* or *The Precipice,* nor is the plot as complicated as are the previous ones.
From a structural standpoint, this novel is not divided into
halves. This makes it possible to give a brief outline of the
plot, and the sub-plot, following which I shall discuss Ainslie's
progress through the first, and Archie MacNeil's through the
second.

Broughton is a coal-mining town in Cape Breton and
Daniel Ainslie, a brilliant doctor hobbled by personal guilt,
has his practice there. His wife, Margaret, is a very attractive,
sensual woman, descended from Loyalists—she does not
understand the Highland temperament, and this has helped
to create a gulf between them. The guilt, however, is much
more the fault of Ainslie, who is unable to show emotion,
including love, without guilt and who is too proud to make
concessions. They never had any children because his work
meant more to him at the time; and then, suddenly, Margaret
found herself unable ever to conceive.

In the town there also lives Molly MacNeil, who has a
young son, Alan. His father, Archie, is a prize-fighter who
has been down in the United States for four years trying to
make a success of his life. He was driven to his profession
and this self-enforced exile by the same combination of pride
and guilt that is the cause of Ainslie's perplexity.

Molly, her husband so long away, succumbs to the advances
of a Frenchman named Louis Camire. And while this affair
is developing, Ainslie's conscience drives him to wish for a
son. Alan is a most intelligent boy, and Ainslie, not out of
love, but to placate his own guilt, tries hard to seduce him
away from his mother. The doctor causes Molly to write and
tell her equally lonely husband that she never wants to see
him again. The upshot is that Ainslie becomes estranged
from Molly and her son, and from his wife more than ever.
Camire is all set to take Molly and Alan off to France.

Then Archie MacNeil, by now a wreck of a man, comes
home. He finds Molly and Camire together, kills them both
with a poker, and dies himself. Ainslie and Margaret get
Alan in the end; through the purgation of soul-searching and

violence, Ainslie finds himself free to love.

There are four characters in this novel who are brilliantly portrayed—Ainslie, Archie MacNeil, his wife and Alan. Because Ainslie is the major one of the four and because his actions in large part determine what happens to the others, one must first look at him.

His problem is manifested by an uncomfortable marriage. His wife Margaret wants "more than anything else" to be able to show him her love physically. Ainslie works long, irregular hours, and in his spare time studies Greek; "Beyond that, he had never been an easy man to love. There seemed to be a diamond in him in place of a heart." [12]

It was only his surface that was hard; inside was a hungry tenderness which she seemed powerless to answer. Inside Dan Ainslie was a humility so basic and profound it frightened her. No matter how good his work might be, she knew it would never be good enough to satisfy him. Not once had it occurred to him how strong was his own personality; how much men and women were moved to try to earn his approval. In his own eyes he was always falling short of an ideal she had never seen clearly enough to understand. He grumbled about the stupidity of others and wounded nearly everyone by his surface rudeness, and of course it never occurred to those he hurt that this was one of his ways of finding fault with himself. [13]

MacLennan's aim is to examine and illuminate these two seemingly contradictory aspects of Ainslie's character, and as the novel moves on he does so.

The revelation is carried out principally through Dr. Dugald MacKenzie, an older colleague and close friend of Ainslie's, who acts almost as a conscience. Ainslie, sad, lonely, estranged from his wife, regards his life as a "memory of striving, straining, heaving the huge rock up the hill with the feeling that if he relaxed for a moment it would become the rock of Sisyphus and roar down the valley bottom again. Was defiance all that remained?" [14] MacKenzie tells him, "You are trying to substitute works for—for what you lack between you. But no man can deliberately exclude his wife from the centre of his life and hope to escape the hounds." [15] "As long as you've been married to Margaret, you've resented her because she hasn't been able to wash away your sense of sin." [16] Ainslie's response to this statement is important: "What on earth are you talking about?" He has not been aware of the nature of the albatross around his neck—he only knows that it is there. Mackenzie explains:

The old man smiled at his own thoughts. "Dan, you haven't forgotten a single word you've ever heard from the pulpit or from your own Presbyterian father. You may think you've rejected religion with your mind, but your personality has no more rejected it than dyed cloth rejects its original colour." MacKenzie's voice became sonorous with irony as he tried to remember Calvin: "Man, having through Adam's fall lost communion with God, abideth evermore under His wrath and curse, except such as He hath out of His infinite loving-kindness and tender mercy, elected to eternal life through Jesus Christ—I'm a Christian, Dan, but Calvin wasn't one and neither was your father. It may sound ridiculous to say, in cold words, that you feel guilty merely because you are alive, but that's what you were taught to believe until you grew up." [17]

Ainslie, although he does not know it at the time, begins a journey toward self-knowledge:

MacKenzie had told him that although he might be an intellectual agnostic, he was an emotional child in thrall to his barbarous Presbyterian past. As he thought this, he felt guilty again. But why? Was there no end to the circle of Original Sin? Could a man never grow up and be free? It was deeper than theory and more personal. There was Margaret—he felt guilty before her, guilty in his soul. Why again? Merely because when he married her, he had been so swayed by sexual desire? As he thought this he saw her anew, as he had seen her the first time, that wonderful, white, firm body so eager for pleasure with him, himself desperate for the joy in her, yet at the same time half afraid and half ashamed. Why again? What was wrong with desire except that within himself it was overpowering and he feared it? Why did he fear it, since she had always been able to satisfy it? Because he had been taught to fear it. Because it led hellwards. But he was a physician, a learned man of forty-two years, and he no longer believed in hell and damnation. No, but he did believe, and believed because it was true, that he had permitted the fables of his childhood to destroy much of Margaret's happiness. So the circle was complete again. Any way he regarded himself, he was guilty, and there was no way out.[18]

One finds MacLennan handling internal revelation with a new ease in this book. Soon after the above talk has taken place, Ainslie is driving home in the night from the hospital, and lonely as he remembers his youth:

The face of his father flashed before his eyes. How could he ever hope to win the kind of struggle such a father had bred into his son? The old Calvinist had preached that life was a constant struggle against evil, and his son had believed him. At the same time, he had preached that failure was a sin. Now the man who had been the boy must ask, How could a successful man be sinless, or a sinless man successful?

Ainslie's body swayed as the wheels hit a rut. He wished he had a son. To work as he did now was senseless. To work for a son's future would give purpose to the universe. He wanted a son who would grow into a learned man and a daughter who would be gentle and admiring of him.[19]

He recalls Mollie MacNeil's son, whom he doesn't really know, but whom he thinks of as remarkable—an intelligent boy with great possibilities, doomed to a life in the coal mines.

Broughton itself has added to the burden of Ainslie's guilt and sadness, for in the collieries a proud people labour for a meagre living. MacKenzie tells him,

"For a man with your imagination Broughton was never the place, Dan. I'm convinced that God himself can never lick the mines. It's a kind of blasphemy, I know—fighting clans going into the blackness of the earth to dig coal. But *you* can't solve the problem."

"There's more to Cape Breton than the mines," Ainslie said at last. "You know that, Dr. Dugald. They're only a—a corruption."

"Yes, there's more here in Cape Breton than that. And each year the best of the island emigrates. We're a dispersed people doomed to fight for lost causes." [20]

Ainslie is an exceptionally brilliant man, a man who could do great things in medical research, and this sorrow for his

race, for their stagnation, evinces itself in a sometimes un-
necessarily harsh brusquenes with the people of Broughton.
Margaret knows why: "It was too frustrating to a mind like
his to be constantly irritated by people he wanted to love and
admire." [21]

But at the same time Ainslie is a compassionate human
being, and MacLennan brings this out particularly well in
chapters six and eight. A young, ignorant Newfoundlander
has lost his hands in an accident. Ainslie operates, and the
tenderness of his emotion in handling this boy, whose life
has been made a shambles, is beautifully transferred to the
reader.

Margaret he cannot get close to, as much as he *wants* to,
and so, to assuage his guilt for her childlessness—and his
own—he plots to steal the affections of another man's son.
One day, alone with Mollie MacNeil and Alan, he tells her,
"It would be a crime for a boy like that to go into the pits."
Watching Mollie, "He knew, as one Highlander always
knows when he sees it in another, that she had quality. She
was incomparably superior to her husband; therefore her
marriage proved that she was excessively malleable. When
he came to this final conclusion he felt ashamed and knew
why, for he realised that if he wished to influence her, he
could do so." [22] Mollie has had a letter from Archie, asking
her and Alan to join him in the United States—he is lonely
and a decisive fight is coming up. Ainslie, of whose opinion
she has some awe, strongly advises her not to go. She writes
and tells Archie that she never wants to see him again.

Not long afterwards, developments come to a head when
Alan goes to hospital for an appendectomy. Ainslie makes a
noticeable fuss over the boy and goes so far as to give him
a private room and asks that the bill be sent to himself.
Ainslie knows that Margaret will strenuously object, that she
"would never forget that he was another man's son" and that
he is deceiving Mollie; but in his emotion, tangled and
possessive, they don't count—he has found a son.

There is was. All of it. It made no difference that Alan was
the child of two people as dissimilar from himself and Margaret as were Archie and Mollie MacNeil. A man's son is the

boy he himself might have been, the future he can no longer attain. For him, Alan was that boy.[23]

Then, once more, Ainslie confides in Dugald MacKenzie —tells him all. Earlier he had broken down and cried and he is ashamed of this, supposes it is a trait inherited from his mother, whom he was taught to regard by his father as weak. But it turns out that MacKenzie knew his parents, knew that his father's ambitious pride had caused him to all but starve his family in order to save money for his three sons' education. And Dr. Dugald rebukes Ainslie for the attitude he has towards his mother, tells him that she starved herself to death in order to keep him alive: "You would do well to honour your father less and your mother more. She was a very loving woman."

Ainslie catches a glimpse of the parallel between what happened with his parents and what is now happening between himself and Mollie MacNeil. "Behind him the old man was saying, 'You aren't looking for a son, Dan. You're looking for God.'"

It took a while for the import of the words to reach him. He felt alone as he had never been alone in his life . . . As his father had denied his mother, so he was trying to deny Alan's mother, to disregard her, to dismiss her as of no importance. And yet the little boy he once had been still longed to be loved by some human being as Alan was loved by her. It was all too confused . . .

When he turned around his face was dark with anger. "You don't understand," he said. "All I want to do is help the boy. Mollie MacNeil is a good woman, but she'll never be more than what she is now, and Alan deserves far better than that. I'm the only one who can help him and nothing is going to stop me. Nothing."[24]

Alan leaves the hospital, and Ainslie makes him eat meals with himself and Margaret—"to build up his strength." Mollie does not like this arrangement, and Margaret resents it. Yet neither woman says anything to Ainslie, each having good reason not to. Then, however, Mollie comes to Margaret and they exchange their fears and doubts. Mollie explains that she wants to go to France with Camire, and take Alan. Margaret, though ashamed of herself for doing so, agrees that this would be best. One is left with a sense of foreboding: "She sensed, without having to put the thought into words since the religion common to Daniel and herself had performed that task for her in childhood, that the essence of sin is a wilful and inextricable involvement of the self in the lives of other people." [25]

When Ainslie discovers that Mollie has, as it were, taken Alan away from him—Margaret tells him why—he rushes off to confront her. But Mollie is adamant, and Ainslie leaves her house without seeing her son. Walking back alone, he finally acknowledges his latest share of guilt, admits to himself that it was he who drove Mollie to extremes with Camire. The Calvinism that was instilled in him when he was just a boy he now sees clearly to be the root of his despair:

Underneath all his troubles, he told himself, lay this ancient curse. He thought desperately of Margaret and desperately of himself, and he knew that it was his fear of the curse which had hobbled his spirit. The fear of the curse had led directly to fear of love itself. They were criminals, the men who had invented the curse and inflicted it upon him, but they were all dead. There was no one to strike down in payment for generations of cramped and ruined lives. The criminals slept well, and their names were sanctified. [26]

He forces himself to believe that there is no God, and that a man can live without love; he finds, for a time, uneasy peace. The only thing left for him to do is to go to Europe and there put his medical skill and ideas to the test of research. Margaret is content that a demon has been driven out of her husband, and there, momentarily, let us leave Ainslie.

Archie MacNeil, when the reader meets him, is in Trenton training for a fight that could, he believes, set him on the road toward the top. Once he was good. But he is now twenty-eight, and his eyes, beetled with scar-tissue, are vulnerable. Still, he is keen on this fight, feels good, wants desperately to win. But the promoter who owns him, realising that he's all but through as a boxer, decides at this crucial time to discard Archie. He leaves him on his own for a week before the fight.

MacNeil is lonely and it is his own fault—but it is also something that he cannot help. He is, MacLennan is saying, a Highlander of proud fighting blood, too proud to work in the mines of Broughton. Mollie has written him—he keeps the old and faded letter—imploring him to return home. He has never answered. MacNeil meets a fellow Cape Bretoner in a Trenton bar who tells him of Mollie and his son—that they want him to return.

"They can say what they God damn well please," Archie said hoarsely, "but I whill not go into the mine again. That iss what she wanted and she iss one of those that know how to make you ashamed of yourself. For the sake of the boy she would make an ox of me, but I saw what she wass after. She iss one of those that whill haff their way by being nice no matter what the hell you do, but by Chesus, it will take more than her, or you either, to get me back to the mine." [27]

It is a poignant scene, this, in the bar; but you cannot feel the weight of it if you don't know Highlanders. MacLennan does:

Archie raised his glass and poured down the drink in a single gulp. Then he felt the haze spread through him and knew he had taken too much, for he was feeling the beginning of the sadness even though it was still daylight. It was not unhappiness such as city people know. It was concerned with no one thing in particular, for it was the primitive sadness of his whole race. He began to hum a song, and as MacLeod recognised the tune he joined him, singing the words in a melancholy cadence. [28]

And the poignancy is increased in the next chapter, as Archie sits down to write to Mollie, begging her to join him: there is a pathetic pride in his signature—*Archie MacNeil from Cape Breton*. This is the letter that Ainslie hears about, and then advises Mollie to forget her husband. So, alone, Archie walks the dirty streets of Trenton.

He lowered his head and walked on, a Highlander lost in the lowlands of the shrewd men. His battered features and huge hands frightened the old lady whom he bumped into as he turned a corner, but he was unconscious of her feeling and failed to notice her surprise at the gentle lilt in his voice when he touched his cap and told her he was sorry.[29]

It must be stressed again that MacLennan is here writing from his cultural consciousness. Ivor Brown, himself a Scot, writes: "Stern and mild! This extraordinary mixture of extremes has been typical of the people who lived there. The Highlander has been both the most ferocious of warriors and the most courteous man of peace. . . . Highland pride could melt to make the perfect man servant, the ghillie of irreproachable manners."[30] One sees these qualities in Archie MacNeil. At one place in these first chapters about MacNeil, a reporter is talking to Archie's trainer:

> "He comes from some place up in Canada, doesn't he?" the reporter said. "Irish, isn't he?"
> "MacNeil's Scotch."
> "That's too bad. The Scotch never seem to get anywhere in this game. The Irish, the Jews, the Negroes, the Italians—sometimes even the Poles. . . ."[31]

If we take "Scotch" to mean Highlander—and this is the author's intention—we have another instance of intuitive awareness of a singular trait of the Highland character. Ivor Brown again:

> The Highlander of history was magnificent, almost irresistible in assault. But he could not organise a victory; he got bored with the business; rear-guard actions did not appeal to his martial romanticism.[32]

In the interval before the fight, Archie gets "bored with the business," succumbs to prostitutes and whisky. Out of shape, he battles his opponent in smothering mid-summer heat and is knocked out, finished. Back in Cape Breton the next morning.

> . . . men talked over the fight on their way down in the cages and behind counters. None of them could understand how a man could be so superior to his opponent and still be beaten like that. They felt the luck must have been against him, a superstition which more or less satisfied them all. It made them feel at one with Archie because they knew that luck was certainly working against themselves.[33]

MacNeil wanders from city to city, a sick man looking for

one more fight which never materialises. He finally gets to
Montreal, works on the docks, and tries desperately to get
a match with the Canadian champion in his class. He is blind
in one eye and the other is going; a kindly French-Canadian
promoter tries to help him, suggests that he go home, and
offers to pay his way. Too proud to take the money, Archie
stumbles dizzily out into the sweltering Montreal streets.
Finally he gets as far as Moncton, climbs on a freight-train,
and heads for home.

The relationship between Mollie MacNeil and her son is
a minor triumph of MacLennan's. He says of Mollie at the
beginning that she is "a woman who has lived for years with
a child and for a child" and her love for Alan, her desire
to do what is best for him, is a compelling undercurrent
throughout the novel. She hates Archie's profession and her
instincts have set her against his leaving Cape Breton; but
she cannot tell Alan her doubts and fears. Alan, at first, does
not know what his father does:

"Mummy?" The boy's face was grave as he forgot about
the ship. "Where is Father now?"

She set her basket down on the sand and the smile left
the corners of her mouth. "But I have told you, Alan—I have
told you over and over again." The smile reappeared to
encourage him. "See if you can remember all by yourself."

"Father has gone out into the world," he said, as if repeat-
ing a lesson.

She clapped her hands. "Now tell me the other thing. Why
has he gone out into the world?"

"He has gone away to do things for us. And when he comes
back everything will be good. We will go into the store and
get whatever we want and people will be proud of us and
we will live in a fine house and be different." [34]

Despite her hatred of his fighting, Mollie knows the real
reason why her husband has gone south; when Alan asks her
whether his father remembers him, Mollie replies: "Archie
MacNeil," she said the name proudly. "It is something to be
the son of the bravest man in all Cape Breton." But Mollie
is torn with misgivings. Archie has not sent any money for
more than a year, and his last postcard is eight months old;
he had said in it that he loved her, but she "aches with

longing." Lonely, as lonely in her own way as Archie and Ainslie are in theirs, she has begun to see Louis Camire, a socialistic, embittered wastrel who is working in Broughton. Alan is too young to comprehend Camire's hold over his mother, which is purely one of physical need.

One day, Mollie takes Alan on a picnic. They go by train and Ainslie is aboard, on his way to an operation. He persuades them to go as far as Louisburg, and there he later joins them. Alan's hunger for knowledge is caught in this scene, as is Mollie's uneasiness at being on equal terms with "The Doctor;" here it is that Ainslie tells her what to write.

MacLennan's special ability to capture a boy's thoughts and actions—we have seen it plainly before in Roddie Wain —is never more evident than in Alan's scenes from Chapter 18 on. At this point, the morning after Archie has lost his fight, Alan overhears his mother and a neighbour speaking:

Alan heard his mother speak again, her voice sounding a wild note that scared him. "Four years, Mr. MacIvor. Four years Alan and I have been alone here. I wrote him a letter to Trenton, but now he will not answer it. Four years! Each time his picture is in the papers I must burn it so Alan will not see what they have done to his face. It is awful, those men he is with. I knew they were awful, and the doctor himself says there are no words for them. It is those men who have changed him."[35]

Mollie leaves the house and Alan, looking for her, comes to the house of Mrs. MacCuish, who gives him a lunch:

"Say your grace before you put that fud into your mouth or it whill poison you."

Alan looked at her wide-eyed, frightened and puzzled.

"Heh!" she cried at him. "And what else would I be expecting but this? You do not know your grace whateffer. Now then, you will say it after me." She fixed her narrow eyes on his. "Most merciful God'—go on, say it now!"

"Most merciful God" Alan repeated.

"I am a miserable sinner and I know I will be damned."

"I am a miserable sinner and I know I will be damned." [36]

She goes on to tell him what sin is, and that "the time whill come when you whill pay, and when you whill remem-

ber everything you haff done, but then it whill be too late
whateffer." A scared Alan leaves this Calvinist hag and roams
off.

That night lying in bed Alan hears Camire and his mother
arguing downstairs. When the Frenchman leaves she comes
up to him, needing someone to unburden herself to, and she
remarks, "It must be beautiful in France. People don't fight
with each other like they do here. I should think maybe we
can go there someday."

Long after she had left him to sleep Alan thought about
what she had said. It was the first time he had ever heard
her talk about going to some other place. At school the
teacher had told them about boys from Cape Breton who had
gone away from home to the States and become famous. But
Alan did not want to go away from home. He wanted his
father to come home instead so he could see him fight and
watch people pay money for a prize and then read about
how famous his father was in the papers.[37]

Equally convincing is Alan's time in hospital. Especially
memorable is his conversation with Bill Blackett, the Newfoundlander whom Ainslie has operated on. In this scene we
notice MacLennan's ear for dialect, and the humour of
Blackett serves to modulate the serious atmosphere of the
story. When Alan goes home from the hospital, "the house
in the miners' row seemed much smaller than he remembered
it, and his mother seemed much younger and even prettier."
She has been sleeping with Camire.

As the freight-train bringing his father home comes round
the Bras d'Or, Alan lies awake in bed. His mother is in the
parlour with Camire, who "had brought a bottle of red wine
when he came and . . . made Alan understand that he
wanted the wine and his mother to himself." The boy is
bewildered. Mollie has by this time come to keep him away
from Ainslie, and Alan feels guilty—"Was it on account of
Mr. Camire that the doctor no longer wanted to see him? . . .
There was an occasional movement in the parlour but the
sound was very faint and he could hardly hear it. Mr. Camire
and his mother were not even talking together." So he lies
there, his thoughts swinging to his father, of whom he is very

proud: "His father was a fighting man, a man so wonderful at fighting that people wrote about him in newspapers, a man so mighty that when Alan had asked if Red Willie MacIsaac could beat him, Angus the Barraman had roared with laughter."

All at once a door opens downstairs. Alan thinks Camire is leaving and goes out on the landing to wait for his mother. Then he hears thuds and grunts in the parlour, his mother screams, and furniture crashes over: "When he reached the lighted square of the parlour door he stopped like a fawn caught in the headlight of a train." His father has come home.

This tragic climax was inevitable. MacLennan has led the reader up to it by the crossed path of Ainslie's private quest and the inexorable downfall of Archie MacNeil. When the bodies have gone to the hospital and Ainslie comes home at last—he had found Alan amid the bloody shambles—he finds Margaret there with him in her arms. Ainslie, finally, breaks down, gives way to his emotions.

MacKenzie arrives and Ainslie confesses to him:

"I killed her as surely as my father killed my mother . . . You told me the truth once and I wouldn't listen. Through arrogance, the both of us. Through total incapacity to understand that in comparison with a loving human being, everything else is worthless."

"Keep a grip on yourself, Dan," MacKenzie said sharply.

"What else have I done all my life but keep a grip on myself?" Ainslie shuddered. "Alan is terrified of me now. He isn't afraid of Margaret at all."

"That's only shock." MacKenzie's shrewd eyes probed his friend's exhausted face. "It was you who found him hiding and he's still terrified by what he saw tonight. It's only shock and it will pass."

Ainslie closed his eyes. "But I love the boy."

MacKenzie rose, set his empty glass beside the untouched one and put his hands on Ainslie's shoulder.

"Yes, Dan. Now I think you do." [38]

In an essay written in 1957, Hugh MacLennan said this: "So I wrote six novels, four of which were published, and when the last was finished I believed I had finally mastered a difficult and complex art." [39] Did he master the art of fiction in *Each Man's Son?* Almost.

The major strength of this book has been discussed above —MacLennan's interpretation of the Highland character and the logical sequence of events which derives from aspects of that character. Daniel Ainslie, Archie, Mollie and Alan Mac-Neil are all characters in the round. Ainslie's searing dilemma is made all the more vivid by two lesser characters—Margaret and Dr. MacKenzie. Through Margaret's feeling of loss, her inability to understand the core of her husband's guilt, and through the wise but firm and natural analysis of Mac-Kenzie, Ainslie is made all the more real—their involvement, as well as Mollie's and Alan's is necessary; without it, Ainslie's search for self-knowledge would never gain impetus.

Critics have found Margaret wanting; they think her as shadowy and vague a figure as Kathleen Tallard. They are right, but one questions whether a fuller, a more alive, wife is really needed for Ainslie. It is, essentially, his story; we are told enough about Margaret's Loyalist background to appreciate her inability to understand her husband's temperament. When the occasion arises, and she must act forcefully —as when Mollie comes to her about Alan—she does so. Perhaps that is enough.

There is, however, one character for whom one has little regard, and that is Camire. He serves his purpose, and is realistic enough, but somehow one cannot reconcile oneself to the presence of such a bizarre type in Broughton. Why not a man from Ontario (or even New Brunswick) instead of a left-wing fanatic from France?

In any event, the debatable weaknesses of these two are more than countered by a colourful gallery of minor figures; Red Willie MacIsaac, Angus the Barraman, Mrs. MacCuish, all the townspeople of Broughton with their sibilant Gaelic intonation, their drunken brawls which act as a respite from the filth of the mines. Through them, MacLennan laces his book with an engaging humour. It would be wrong to regard these Cape Breton Highlanders simply as "characters"— MacLennan's descriptions of them are realistic, from their accents down to their Calvinistic habits: "They cooked all the food for Sunday on the day before, put it on plates and the tables, and he even saw to it that they filled all the glasses in the house with water on Saturday night, so that not a tap was turned in the MacGillivray house on the Sabbath." [40] One is reminded of Hardy's vivid gallery of minor figures—humorous, lively, and not idealised. Also, there are the tough, sour men who run Archie's life in the United States, Sam Downey and Charlie Moss—they fit just as well into their environment as the Cape Bretoners do into theirs.

In short, MacLennan's technique of characterisation is excellent—nowhere else has he managed to capture and depict such a wide range of human emotions.

Heretofore we have seen the settings to be in places almost overpowering, something which can, and at times does, make the characters seem almost insignificant. In *Each Man's Son* one never has this feeling. The characters, although shaped by it, are more important than their environment, move within it surely and naturally.

MacLennan's description of Archie training in Trenton and of the fight itself are easily among the very best this writer has ever come across about boxing. MacLennan knows his sports, and he knows how men connected with them act and think. Here and there in the book one finds the isolated vague or fuzzy sentence, but there are so few of these that they count for nothing. MacLennan's style is nearly impeccable. Our interest is centred on Broughton, but when we are switched to Archie's scenes we feel the changes to be smooth and necessary.

The plot builds up steadily and inevitably and our involvement with Ainslie and the MacNeils is heightened by an increasing tension. But there is one flaw that is very noticeable, and almost an echo of the superfluous part of the introduction; it occurs just after Alan has gone home from the hospital—the opening paragraphs of Chapter 23:

If God looked down on them that summer, the kind of God their ministers told them about, He must have been well pleased for by summer's end all of them except Alan were conscious of their sins. Longing to do their best, they had discovered there is no best in this world. Yearning for love, they had found loneliness. Eager to help one another, they had made each other wretched. Dreaming of better lives, they had become totally discontented with the lives they led.

If an omnipotent and interested God looked down on them that summer, irony must have been one of His pleasures. For here in Cape Breton were these innocent ones, eager to make themselves worthy of the great world of Europe from which their ancestors had been driven long ago; and there across the sea was that great world of Europe, enjoying the final summer of its undisturbed arrogance. For this was the year before 1914.[41]

This unnecessary and annoying intrusion by the author is depressingly like the grandiloquent last paragraph of *Two Solitudes*.

One critic has evaluated *Each Man's Son* in terms of Greek tragedy.[42] There is no denying the classical influence upon MacLennan or the fact that its specifications for tragedy may be imposed here, but another interpretation is as plausible. The over-all tone of the book is sombre; MacLennan, as has been pointed out, was writing about a part of himself when he composed it. He was unburdening himself of a part of his own spirit, and that spirit had its origins not in Greece but in Kintail. The book is, to use a spelling MacLennan would himself insist upon, "Scotch." Reading it, one is reminded of *Tunes of Glory* (1956), an excellent novel by the Scottish writer James Kennaway. It, too, is a tragedy, and there, as in *Each Man's Son,* the terrible finish derives from the converging paths of two men, both Highlanders, guilt-ridden and proud.

In conclusion, it may be said once more that *Each Man's Son* is the best of MacLennan's novels. Its weaknesses are, when all is said, minor—they are all but forgotten as one is struck by the lifting power of the story. However, in the final analysis, it must be conceded that few readers will appreciate MacLennan's faithful delineation of the Highland character in *Each Man's Son*. To many, the novel will seem, perhaps, too narrow in scope, too involved with what is apparently an isolated, almost grotesque spiritual phenomenon. Others, one feels, will appreciate the controlled emotional fullness of the book without really understanding it. Neither attitude should be permitted to detract from the acclaim that is this novel's due.

CHAPTER SIX

∿ THE WATCH THAT ENDS THE NIGHT

The Watch that Ends the Night is, in Canada, a celebrated novel. Malcolm Ross was inspired to say after reading it, "I would not trade MacLennan for a legion of beatniks or a whole flotilla-full of angry young men."[1] George Woodcock had praise somewhat more concrete: "MacLennan is a craftsman writer in the good sense . . . he is nearer than any other contemporary Canadian writer to being a master of fiction."[2] *The New York Times'* reviewer also waxed enthusiastic— ". . . this is a better novel than he has written before;"[3] and in fact, the novel was on the best-seller list of the *Times Book Review* for eighteen weeks—so its acclaim was, much more so than was the case with MacLennan's previous books, international in scope. For all that, it is a disappointing novel. Its success can be attributed to a simple, but attractive, theme and a fabulous hero.

MacLennan spent six years writing *The Watch That Ends the Night* and when he had finished it he clearly believed that he had accomplished something special. He had, he tells us, "a sudden realisation" in 1951 "that the traditional novel was failing in its function:"

Around this time, it seemed to me, as it seemed to the educated public, that the basic human conflict was "within" the individual. But how to find an artistic form for this concept? That was the question. Certainly the novelists failed who wrote clinically; they absolutely failed to purge the soul of pity and terror, which is art's supreme function. When I began *The Watch That Ends the Night* I was at least clear on that score. I would *not* write a clinical book. But somehow I was going to write a book which would not depend on character-in-action, but on spirit-in-action. The conflict here, the essential one, was between the human spirit of Everyman and Everyman's human condition.

In order to find an accurate fictional form for this concept of life, I wrote millions of words and postponed the publication of *The Watch That Ends the Night* for some eight years. Or rather, I spent more than six years learning how to shape a new bottle for a new kind of wine.[4]

This terminating declaration is bewildering. MacLennan did change his basic, omniscient-author technique, but nothing really new emerged; he simply gave us a first-person narrator and a structure that is built around the flashback. Structurally, the novel is satisfying but hardly original. In handing over his omniscience to a protagonist, MacLennan effects both good and bad results; one is relieved of MacLennan's editorial intrusions, but the narrator himself is never able to give us the necessary depth of insight into other figures of the novel.

The Watch That Ends the Night is MacLennan's most ambitious book, for, besides changing his style, he is attempting to explore, as he puts it, "spirit-in-action," the development of a person through conflict with the eternal human condition. With one partial exception the characters are not, as some earlier ones have been, puppets of a rather narrow theme; nor are they confined to the limitations of a sequestered environment—they act out their lives in a wide, chiefly cosmopolitan milieu. At the same time, MacLennan makes the novel something of a melting-pot for ideas and obsessions of his, a number of which we have seen before—the guilt-complex of the Thirties generation; aspects of Canada's struggle for self-knowledge; the theme itself—the wonder of the beauty of life. It should be said, too, that the best-seller appeal of the theme owes a great deal to MacLennan's personal experience, as Dorothy Duncan died under circumstances approximating those which wear down Catherine, the novel's heroine; and this makes it all the more natural for George Stewart, the narrator, to sound, in some places, a lot like Hugh MacLennan.

The story is built around three main characters, George, Catherine, whom he has loved from youth and whom he

eventually marries, and Jerome Martell, the soulful superman who marries her first. It is, regrettably, these three
people who bring the book to its knees—George because he
never engages one's sympathy as he should, Catherine because
she never comes alive, and Jerome because he defies credibility. Their triangular relationship is the substance of the
plot.

When the book opens in 1950, George is a part-time
lecturer at McGill. He and Catherine have been married
since the war-years, when word had gotten back to Montreal
that Jerome had been tortured to death by the Nazis. Only
now, with time eradicating the burden of his memory, is
George beginning to attain contentment and confidence.
Catherine, recurrently succumbing to a rheumatic heart
condition which has been with her since youth, is his to care
for, his own responsibility; Sally, Catherine's college-age
daughter by Jerome, looks to George as her father; he is
happy in his work. Then he answers an apparently innocuous
phone-call and hears Jerome's voice at the other end, the
voice of a man whom he "had thought dead for a decade."
This blow staggers him into a recollection of the past which
forms the bulk of the novel.

George is a thoroughly realistic character, but from the
first he alienates the reader. Initially, this is because he is
made to shoulder, in a tiresomely self-pitying fashion, Mac-
Lennan's own guilt-complex about the Thirties; he is a
"scarred" product of the Depression:

I have never felt safe. Who of my age could, unless he was
stupid? Quite a few people thought me successful, but in my
own eyes I was no more successful than the old Greek who
pushed boulders up the hill knowing they would tumble down
the moment they reached the top. Some people thought me
calm, but inside I knew I was not. . . . The young have the
necessary self-confidence and ignorance to feel mature, and
that is why I like them so much better than I like my own
generation. Was there ever a crowd like ours? Was there
ever a time when so many people tried, so pathetically, to
feel responsible for all mankind? Was there ever a generation
which yearned to belong, so unsuccessfully, to something
larger than themselves?[5]

The suggestion here of self-deprecation mushrooms into a jejune string of related revelations:

I'm not a man with much self-confidence and when I was young I took it for granted that nobody respected me or paid me any attention. When I was young I was just another of those people who are around, for I had, and still have, a clumsy body of which I was never proud and when I was young I was timid.[6]

I was too clumsy to ever be an athlete but I had always enjoyed walking and physical exercise . . . But I was certainly not a man people notice in a crowd. I was no Jerome Martell, whom everyone had noticed wherever he was.[7]

Myself was the person who wished he was a hero, and had been born clumsy and had grown up without much courage.[8]

"It's not as if I was any first prize," I said.[9]

I was only seventeen and I had never had any confidence in myself.[10]

I was an incurable product of the depression. In my heart I never believed that a job would last.[11]

And what a generation I belonged to, where so many of the successful ones, after trying desperately to hitch their wagons to some great belief, ended up believing in nothing but their own cleverness.[12]

These excerpts are drawn only from the first hundred pages. But this self-pitying, confessional note recurs right to the end.

George has good reason for being as he is—he has weak, eccentric parents who lose their money, an aunt who domineers the family, and (lest we forget) his own clumsiness. However, such a character, with his whipped-dog attitude, is not the sort toward whom a reader is attracted—not unless he outgrows his weakness and redeems himself in our eyes. George never quite succeeds.

When, as a young man, Catherine wants him to sleep with her, he is afraid to—"I trembled and was afraid not merely as a boy who fears to make a girl pregnant, but because I was not yet a man."[13] Later he works at a number of dreary jobs, graduates from university at twenty-seven, loses faith in himself, religion, and the "integrity of human society" during the Depression, and finally ends up teaching at Water-

loo, a boys' boarding school. Whenever possible, he spends
the weekends in Montreal. A friend of his tells him,

"You know, George, you're that very rare thing, a perfect
specimen. You're middle class to the bone. You're a nice guy.
All you want is a nice little wife and a nice little apartment
and a nice little job, and yet you hang around with these
hot-shots that hang around me. You're about as revolutionary as Stanley Baldwin." [14]

George does little to discourage this assertion. He does
engage in an affair, but as is always the case with MacLennan
vs. Sex the particulars are decorously skirted. Eventually he
runs into Catherine again—it's been twelve years—and with
her is Martell; after this he sees them regularly:

My own position with the Martells was at once peculiar
and simple. Jerome was unconscious of jealousy and he liked
me, as I liked him, yet I doubt if he ever thought about me
when I was not in his company. I desired Catherine in
addition to loving her, but it takes two to make desire jump
the spark-gap, and in those days all her desire was polarised
to her husband. She used to tease me and tell me I ought to
marry, and several times . . . she introduced me to girls she
thought would make good wives, and in a motherly way she
professed to feel responsible for my future. [15]

Still futilely loving Catherine, George actually comes to
look upon Jerome as a father: ". . . not my actual father but
for a time in the Thirties, when I was spiritually and emotionally fatherless, I had virtually allowed him to become
so." [16] When Jerome swings off to the Spanish Civil War and
is afterwards reported killed, George, who had been padding
furtively along after her, is finally able to marry Catherine.
He gains some stature, but this is a brief interval, for very
soon we are brought back to the beginning, to Jerome's
return from the dead. Catherine suffers a shock from her
first husband's reappearance, and quickly comes close to
death. George despairs: "My subconscious began to scream
at me: Let her die. Let her go. End this." But Jerome saves
her, and goes on his way, leaving George with a new philosophy of life, a renewed will to live.

All the way, then, the narrator, the ostensible hero as it
were, is a broken reed. MacLennan deliberately made him

so, conceivably because such a man, essentially weak and lacking in confidence, is MacLennan's conception of "Everyman"—it is on such a man that Jerome's revelatory sunburst has the greatest impact, the greatest meaning. This is all very well provided the reader sympathises with George; but what attraction he does have is annulled by his ever-present self-pity and by his fawning dependence upon Jerome and Catherine. In short, he is not the sort of man one chooses to identify with; consequently his ultimate regeneration is liable to be taken less seriously than it should be.

Catherine is the motivating figure in the novel, the force which attracts both George and Jerome and which shapes their lives. She talks and paints, has a sensual, "queen-like" aura about her, and battles valiantly against impending death; but one never really knows much about her, and this is because all of our impressions are those which George relays in the course of his narration—too narrow a view, and one prohibitive of exploring the intricacies of her mind. In a way, one is reminded of MacLennan's failure to impress Lucy Cameron's astounding qualities upon the reader; here the same thing is true—Catherine floats through the novel inspiring her lovers to heights of rhetoric and just about everyone gets a chance to remark upon her sterling worth; but one has simply to rely upon their word for it, because she steadfastly hovers in the middle distance and does not come to life.

At one point George tells us what we should look for in this woman he worships:

Her fate was that rheumatic heart of hers. Her strength, her essence, her mystery in which occasionally I had almost drowned—this I can only call her spirit, and I don't use the word in a sentimental sense. Far from it. For to me this has become the ultimate reality, so much so that I think of this story not as one conditioned by character as the dramatists understand it, but by the spirit. A conflict, if you like, between the spirit and the human condition. . . . Catherine had more of this mysterious thing than anyone I ever knew with one exception, and the exception was Jerome Martell. Is this another way of saying that she was not easy to live with? Or is it another way of saying that it was so impossible for me to imagine myself living without her that—without realising I did so—I sometimes dreaded her because of my dependence on her?

Yet I loved her. She was my rock, she was my salvation, but I also loved her for herself. When she moved like a queen I was proud. When she smiled like a little girl I melted.

Have I described Catherine? I don't think so. Probably I have only described myself.[17]

And this is the trouble throughout.

There is one brief section of the book in which Catherine seems something more than a shade. In the summer of their youth, when she and George fall in love, she becomes quite real as she explains to him that, because of her heart, she can never bear children; but she refuses to be crushed by this order and tries—as we have seen—without success to make love to George. Then she goes on to McGill, marries Jerome, and later George, and, in the closing stages of the novel, is racked by successive attacks. These inspire, for one thing, persistent and embarrassing orotundity on George's part:

Suddenly it seemed to me that we were almost isolated by her fate. I became aware that some of our friends regarded Catherine's plight with awe. They spoke of her courage and outward cheerfulness, they were kind and thoughtful, but it must have been painful at times for them to think about us.

They, too, were nearing early middle age. They were reaching the place where the final enemy ceases to be a mere word. They had seen his tracks in the forest, they had heard his horns in the night, they had come upon the traces of his fires. They knew he was planting his little fifth columns in their arteries and valves and organs and the cigarettes they smoked and the tensions under which they lived. A few of them looked at Catherine, I sometimes thought, as I myself had looked at some small, defenceless country near to Hitler's Germany in the years when Hitler seemed as omnipotent as fate. She would get it first. She, still so young in years, was a preview of what lay in wait for all.[18]

But chiefly, Catherine's illness is the vessel of the theme:

Now in her final phase what I used to think of as her

character ceased to matter in Catherine; her character almost
disappeared into her spirit. The Catherine I knew and loved
was still present and visible, was even fun to be with. But
the essential Catherine—what now was the essential Catherine—sometimes seemed to me like the container of a life-
force resisting extinction.[19]

In fact it becomes clear as the novel progresses that
MacLennan is eluding the responsibility of making Catherine, his heroine, a real person; she is almost solely the
torch-bearer of his philosophy: "Every fortnight or so she
changed the picture which hung on the wall facing the foot
of my bed, and when I woke in the dawn there this thing
was, this expression—not of Catherine but of love of life
itself which in her had become so intense as to be almost
impersonal." [20] She is, when all is said, an idea and not a
vital character. One who remembers that key part of Mac-
Lennan's dictum for the satisfying novel—". . . it must make
the reader a part of the world of the novelist's creation, and
this it does by creating fictional characters more real than
the reader's personal friends"—can only suppose that he
deliberately avoids, or fails in, living up to his own com-
mandment.

Such an opinion is reinforced by the character of Jerome
Martell. As if to over-compensate for the unreal Catherine,
Jerome is shaped to many times real life size. He is born
and brought up, a bastard perhaps, in a lumber camp on
a branch of the Miramichi in which his immigrant mother
is the cook. She is murdered by a berserk lover, and the boy
escapes to Newcastle in a canoe. He jumps a freight to
Moncton, where a kindly clergyman and his wife—the Martells—who are childless, decide to adopt him, and they take
him to live in a Halifax manse. He becomes a brilliant student, then goes to war at seventeen and is a hero—"I was
too good a soldier in the war, George. . . . I killed eleven men
with the bayonet, George." But due to the religious upbringing his foster-parents gave him he is riddled with guilt,
and a young Jew persuades him to blame war on the
capitalist system. He decides to become a doctor, goes to
McGill, and ends up practising surgery in Montreal.

He is a burly, powerful man with "a small blaze of gray on his temple." The first time George saw him

He dropped his cigarette and turned to crush it with his heel, and under the close fit of his dinner jacket a pack of shoulder-muscle shifted and I remembered that Adam Blore had called him a stallion.

Physically ruthless—that was my first thought. But an instant later this impression disappeared. For an usher approached Jerome with a message, and when he turned to read it I saw his face full front and the eyes were wide, intelligent and young. The mouth was sensual but it was also broad and strong; the cheek bones were high and forceful and the features were disciplined. In any crowd I would have recognised that for a doctor's face.[21]

One may dispute this latter proclamation but Jerome, being a doctor, fits right into MacLennan's category of the heroic. He is, to put it mildly, adept at almost anything, be it sex, surgery, or sport. Jerome, George tells us, "had always been a man who lived passionately because that was the only way he had been able to function." His proposal to Catherine carries (to absurdity) a suggestion of this trait: "'Catherine, you're going to marry me and I'm going to make you pregnant and you're going to have at least one child and you're not going to die for a long time. At least you're not going to die till you've had a chance to use a lot of that life of yours.' . . . Sally's birth came close to killing Catherine, but her vast will to live combined with Jerome's force pulled her through."[22] Martell's "force" is quite a remarkable phenomenon. Jack Christopher, "one of Jerome's various protegés," did not know whether to go into business or medicine: ". . . Jerome's enthusiasm had fired him. Now he was hesitating between entering practice in internal medicine and doing work in endocrinology. It was typical of Jerome that he had advised him to try both."[23] Jerome decided that "old George" has a hidden ability for radio announcing, and the man he sends him to see has his own bit to add to the body of Martellian folklore: "He's an amazing man. I've never known anyone like him for discovering a flair in a person the person doesn't know he has."[24] For George, Jerome is not only a "substitute father,"

but an idol: ". . . Jerome—I really came to believe this—
could never belong to any particular group of human beings;
he belonged to humanity itself." [25]

The central event of the novel—as opposed to the pervasive undercurrent of Catherine's plight—is Jerome's deser-
tion of his wife and daughter to go to the Spanish Civil War.
A humanitarian and an idealist, his guilt for the 1914-18
conflict is reinforced by the Depression. "How," he asks
George, "can anyone lead a private life now? Anything to
break the system that causes these things, George. Anything!" He becomes, after George has met him, increasingly
obsessed with politics: "This was a time in which you were
always meeting people who caught politics just as a person
catches religion. It was probably the last time in this century
when politics in our country will be evangelical, and if a
man was once intensely religious, he was bound to be wide
open to a mood like that of the Thirties." [26] Jerome neglects
Catherine and takes a Communist mistress—Norah Blackwell—but Catherine understands—"He thinks that in this
Spanish war he has a chance to make recompense by saving
life." He attends a Communist rally, at which his impulsive
temperament is used by the organisers for prestige value, a
riot breaks out, and the next morning his picture is splashed
in the papers. Fired from his hospital as a result of this
caper, he is free to go to Spain, and George, Catherine and
Sally watch him sail away—as the ship pulls out, Norah
appears beside him on the deck.

He fights with the Loyalists, is captured, goes from one
prison camp to another, is tortured along the way, and ends
up in China, where he has a religious revival:

"One day I woke up and Jesus himself seemed to be in
the cell with me and I wasn't alone. He wasn't anyone I
had ever known before. He wasn't the Jesus of the churches.
He wasn't the Jesus who had died for our sins. He was simply
a man who had died and risen again. Who had died outwardly as I had died inwardly." [27]

The Chinese let him go, and after practising medicine for
a year in Hong Kong he comes home.

His return causes Catherine's relapse. Two other doctors

do all they possibly can for her, but the situation borders on the hopeless until Jerome takes a hand. George (who has not yet seen him) resents this, and storms into his wife's room, sees Jerome tending her, and hates him—"Now he was back. Years of concentration camps, of beatings and starvings and hatings and killings and torturings—there he was like the memory of the human race back beside her for the end, and I thought he looked like a vulture." This impression, however, is immediately dissolved as George looks into Jerome's "Rembrandt"-like eyes:

I had never in my life seen an expression like his. His face seemed white, very lined but the lines finely drawn, the eyes very large. His whole face seemed transparent. And in his eyes was an expression new and uncanny. They seemed to have seen everything, known everything, suffered everything. But what came out of them into me was light, not darkness. A cool, sweet light came out of them into me then. It entered me, and the murderous feeling went out, and I was not afraid any more.[28]

Jerome, mind you, has not performed an operation, he has only sat beside her, but his "unique healing powers" have, somehow, been transferred to Catherine and she revives. George cannot see the point, for she will only have more attacks, will die soon anyway. But the revenant puts his hand on George's shoulder, as it were, and reveals the truths of his private philosophy—she must, Jerome assures him, "live her own death." George is to build a shell around himself:

"What do you mean—a shell?"
He looked at me and suddenly his face became absolutely clear, his eyes all-seeing like Rembrandt's, and he said with an absolute simplicity:
"Death. The shell is death. You must crawl inside of death and die yourself. You must lose your life. You must lose it to yourself."
"What are you talking about?" [29]

Jerome goes on to explain, and George undergoes regeneration—

All of us is Everyman and this is intolerable unless each of us can also be I. What is the struggle worth? How measure a thing like that in terms of ordinary value? Van Gogh painted alone and in despair and in madness and sold one picture in his entire life. Millions struggled alone, unrecognised, and struggled as heroically as any famous hero. Was it worthless? I knew it wasn't—

as Jerome intones, " 'Jesus said, I am the resurrection and the life.' He died in order to prove it and He rose in order to prove it. His spirit rose. He died in order to live. If He had not died, He would not have lived." Silence for a long time. 'Kate will live, and so will you'." [30] Then Jerome, having selflessly redeemed himself and having saved Catherine and George, disappears into the west.

Jerome is impossible to believe in and in his own way he bids fair to be more unreal than Catherine. His life is that of a Hollywood hero—the rescued waif who makes good, who becomes an exceptional student, athlete, war-hero, super-surgeon, lover, stud, father-figure, fount of inspiration, idealist, revolutionary, martyr, and guru. Such a conglomeration of abilities and experiences stuns one who comes to realistic fiction expecting his heroes to be cast in the human mould. MacLennan gives Jerome valid background reasons for his many transformations, but neither these nor occasionally forceful and realistic dialogue is enough to keep him on the level of the credible. Only at one time in the novel does Jerome seem thoroughly believable and that, significantly enough, is during his boyhood—MacLennan's achievement with Roddie Wain and Alan MacNeil is carried over.

Nonetheless, Jerome had to be a major element in the novel's success. One suspects that a great many middle-aged women bought the book; they tend to be attracted to grey-templed, virile doctors, all the more so if the doctor was a member of their own generation and, to boot, abandoned his wife and child only to return in the end and pull her back from the gates of death. *The Watch That Ends the Night* becomes, because of Jerome Martell, an amalgam of the realistic and the "escapist" forms of fiction. It has been argued that MacLennan modelled Martell on Dr. Norman Bethune, and that Jerome is therefore credible. This seems to me to be beside the point. MacLennan may have had Bethune in mind, but his *method* of presenting Jerome—particularly to the reader who has never heard of Bethune—makes any direct relationship between the two less than relevant.

The plot, which is plausible enough in main outline— George's quest for Catherine, her battle for life, Jerome's departure and return—suffers as a consequence of the leading characters, and these leading characters suffer because of the pompous gushing dialogue which is assigned them. If Catherine is nearly intangible, if George is faintly contemptible and Jerome is a superman, one cannot be blamed for losing interest in what happens to them.

There are two other aspects of this book that can be labelled as weak. In a few places, George slips into something closely resembling MacLennan's own didacticism:

While the war thundered on, Canada unnoticed grew into a nation at last. This cautious country which had always done more than she had promised, had always endured in silence while others reaped the glory—now she became alive and to us within her excitingly so. . . . The war thundered on and the Thirties became a memory. I spent a winter in Halifax directing a series of scripts describing some aspects of the navy which then, without anyone seeming to be aware of it, was carrying on sixty percent of the convoy duty on the Atlantic.[31]

But most of George's observations serve as appropriate illuminations of events and situations in the novel. Also, occasionally, MacLennan is guilty of turgid or slipshod writing. Silence is "abrupt and profound as the end of the world;" an act is "done with the silence of animals killing each other in the dark"—in fact, animals are not quite that stoical; rabbits, just to take an example, usually scream when they are attacked. However, generally speaking, the descriptive passages are commendable.

If the three major figures of *The Watch That Ends the Night* are, in their several ways, failures, the minor characters are not. MacLennan has a special gift for describing eccentrics. One remembers George's father with his crossbow, his dogs ("all named after British admirals and generals"), his preposterous inventions and war-games. And, of course, the crusty Dr. Bigbee:

"Bowels," said the Doctor. "Give 'em plenty of time to move 'em. The secret of a good school's a happy boy, and the secret of a happy boy's a comfortable intestine." [32]

With a crash the Doctor dropped both feet to the ground and rose towering among his birds, and with an expression disconcertingly roguish he pointed his finger at me and wagged it.

"Stewart, you're the first native, I mean the first man not from home we've ever had here. So go in and win." [33]

Shatwell, George's colleague at Waterloo—public-school man, Sandhurst, The Army, dabbler in raisins, teak, jute, rubber, and women; the Rev. Giles Martell, kindly, goat-bearded, addicted to rum and eloquence:

"That female standing in receipt of custom for food which is both fly-blown and over-priced denied me a tray. But I insisted. I even pointed to a tray in her lair, and after a time she yielded, and here it is, so we shall all breakfast together." [34]

Most of the other minor characters more than hold their own. Sally is very real—haunted by bitter memories of her father, intelligent, lively, compassionate, openly happy about her love for the "shaggy" Alan Royce. She is a convincing spokesman for her generation. George's Aunt Agnes is a more unpleasant version of Aunt Maria Wain and Jane Cameron —cold, domineering, obsessed with running other people's lives. Adam Blore, a friend of George's who claims to be a sculptor and who sells carpets in Eaton's for a living is effectively portrayed as a member of the Thirties' *avant-garde:*

"Yes, you must really read Céline. Have you gone into the public lavatory of a New York subway lately? One of those places where the unemployed sleep on the ledges above the urinals? That's what Céline's work smells like. By God, but he's got integrity!" [35]

Norah Blackwell, the leftist "nymphomaniac" who captures Jerome is believable, and so is her cuckold of a husband, Harry—a pitiful "pear-shaped" figure who stumbles dully but irately through the novel seeking revenge on Jerome. The one thing that brings all these lesser figures to life more than anything else, in this instance, is MacLennan's competent, sometimes inspired, handling of dialogue—but of course this makes all the more glaring the deficiency of the leading characters.

Perhaps the foremost attribute of the book is MacLennan's descriptive analysis of diverse situations, institutions, and places and his skill in merging them into the flow of the story.

Waterloo School, with its staff of itinerate Englishmen, its motto—'Let the French Beware!'—its staring mob of beasts, fowl, and Admirals of the Red and the Blue, and, above all, its fantastic and memorable head-master, is a delightful diversion from the mainstream of the book. One is inevitably reminded of Evelyn Waugh's Llanabba Castle in *Decline and Fall* and wishes that MacLennan would some-day turn his hand to such a novel.

We have seen the author's ability at writing sequences of action; when compared with the Halifax explosion or Archie MacNeil's fight, Jerome's escape from the lumber camp is up to par. This narrative of suspense is, in Part Five, coupled with fine descriptive passages on the New Brunswick bush and what almost surely is the town of Newcastle. Equally good are the descriptions of Montreal. That city is the cen-tral setting of *The Watch That Ends the Night* and Mac-Lennan, who has made it his home, is in love with the place:

. . . we stepped outside and there from the front of the Arts Building was downtown Montreal like a fleet at anchor in an arctic port with all its lights on and the smoke going straight up. The campus was dark with its elm fountains lean and bare, but long rhomboids of light from the library windows fell across the snow and I saw students passing through them with their breath puffing out and heard their heels creaking on the packed snow.[36]

Permeating the novel is MacLennan's socio-historical analysis of the Thirties. One may feel that George is perhaps too obsessed in identifying himself with his generation, but considering the situation in which he is caught up and the character MacLennan has given him, it is at least not an impossible attitude to take. The Depression contributes to his insecurity, it strikes fire to Jerome's dormant guilt-

complex, pressures his eviction from his practice, his aban-
donment of his wife and child, and his ultimate possession
of mystical power. Still, MacLennan's examination of this
era adds nothing to what we already know. He never writes
with the complete insight of, say, Dos Passos; instead, he
trundles out the time-worn scenes of a faculty-gathering and
a communist rally. Despite the author's repeated protesta-
tions of guilt for his generation, he never makes clear to the
reader the roots of that guilt, the "sickness" of the society of
the day. In places, MacLennan's wistful head-shaking turns
to a prophetic didacticism which has not stood time's test:
"The 1930's was the last time for so many things; it was
certainly the last time in which college professors could believe themselves capable of planning the future of humanity." [37]
One has only to think of Kennedy's men—Bundy, Schlesinger,
et al—or of the academic involvement in the Viet-Nam up-
roar, and MacLennan's pedagogy seems pompous indeed.

Lastly, one must return to the theme, to the doomed
Catherine's struggle for life and George's recognition of the
splendour of this desire. Although the characters who enact
the theme are open to criticism, MacLennan's sincerity can
never be in doubt.

Like Catherine, Dorothy Duncan learned to paint during
her illness and she, too, died of a rheumatic heart after a
very long fight. In his essay, "Christmas without Dickens,"
MacLennan tells of how he spent time "in the hospital wondering whether my wife would live or die."

The struggle had been going on for days, each day harder
than the one before. It was a fair Christmas, but I entered it
with a foreboding I have never known before or since. Strain
and imagination were telling. Everyone I passed, even beautiful girls, I seemed to be seeing as though they were old,
their flesh shrunken as in the hour of their death. [38]

And in *The Watch That Ends the Night* we read,

I came out to a beautiful day, the streets full of people
looking happy because the first breath of spring was in the
air, but I saw them all as they would appear in the hour of
their death. A lovely, laughing girl I saw as a rotted corpse
filled with writhing, white worms. [39]

The essay:

I went into the hospital and the nurse's whisper was not reassuring. In the room I met with bare recognition. It was the same sight that had become so familiar: the tubes, the bottle dripping its liquid into the splinted arm, the rattle of desperate breathing. I sat down and time ticked on, empty and without significance.[40]

The novel:

After a while a nurse appeared and told me I could see Catherine, but only for a moment.

If you are familiar with the aftermaths of major surgery you know what I saw when I entered the room: a tiny form on a white bed, two splinted arms with an intravenous needle in one and a transfusion needle in the other, a gaping mouth through which the breath rasped and a tube protruded, another tube draining the wound hidden by the dressings. An unnatural warmth, the warmth of a snakehouse, pervaded the room.[41]

The essay:

Then suddenly I sat upright with the feeling that something had brushed me lightly and passed. Now, though everything was the same even to the sound of the breathing, the room felt different and an enormous pressure slid away and seemed to sink into the floor.[42]

The novel:

"Just before you came in," I heard him say, "just before you came in I was sitting there. And I felt death brush me as it went out of the room."[43]

In both pieces of writing there is a similar exuberance following the recovery. MacLennan was not making up a fanciful religious message in The Watch That Ends the Night; he was telling with conviction of a private experience that he felt compelled to pass on. "Could I or could I not—could she or could she not—" asks George, "believe that this struggle had any value in itself?" The answer is simple, but eloquent:

So the final justification of the human plight—the final vindication of God himself, for that matter—is revealed in a mystery of the feelings which understand, in an instant of revelation, that it is of no importance that God appears in-

different to justice as men understand it. He gave life. He
gave it. Life for a year, a month, a day or an hour is still a
gift. The warmth of the sun or the caress of the air, the
sight of a flower or a cloud on the wind, the possibility even
for one day more to see things grow—the human bondage
is also the human liberty. . . . to feel the movement of light
flood the darkness of self—even for an instant—is the most
beautiful experience anyone can ever know. And millions
have known it.[44]

Millions may have known this experience, but for how many
has it had the enduring healing power with which MacLennan invests it? The hungry, diseased masses of any century
have, by and large, accepted life with more of a dulled resigna-
tion than anything else. Clearly, the majority of men (Mac-
Lennan's "Everyman") have faced the human condition without consciously having been aware of their "human spirit."
Nonetheless, MacLennan's lesson of "spirit-in-action" is an
admirable philosophy, and one suspects that many readers
of this novel have been deeply moved by the way in which
MacLennan shares with them his hard-won belief.

Had MacLennan made Jerome a plausible human being,
The Watch That Ends the Night would have been a much
better novel. Catherine's frailty as a character would not be
enough to unduly cripple the book, and George would not
have been dwarfed by Jerome's swollen vitality. It is hard
to imagine how a man who laboured so conscientiously and
long over something which he needed to express could himself believe—for he must have done—in a character who is
so recognisably a ruinous force.

So, in this, his latest novel but one, MacLennan still fails
to achieve "a whole which is harmonious." There is a "mystery"—of sorts—and it may well be that the uncontrolled
depth of feeling in the book is essentially Celtic in its inspiration and expression. Finally, although chaotic and over-abun-
dant, there is a fullness and variety in *The Watch That Ends
the Night* that we have not seen before. But the book is,
when all is said, a disappointing achievement for the Canadian "master of fiction."

CHAPTER SEVEN

~ RETURN OF THE SPHINX

MACLENNAN'S latest novel, *Return of the Sphinx* (1967), is, more than anything else, a sequel to *Two Solitudes*. The earlier book ended with a hopeful prediction that this divided country was finally "becoming herself" and was stepping forward with new-found confidence into the future.

But the future has turned out to be both disappointing and full of danger, and *Return of the Sphinx* reflects its author's disillusionment with the state of the world in general and with the seemingly insoluble French-English problem in this country. The pervading theme of the novel is the unchanging capacity of men to do themselves—and their world—lasting injury. Separatist mania in Quebec is the principal manifestation of this theme in the story.

Alan Ainslie, whom we met as a boy in *Each Man's Son*, and Daniel, his son by a French-Canadian wife, Constance (who was killed in a traffic accident before the novel opens), are the protagonists; the conflict between them is the core of the story. Alan, the Minister for Cultural Affairs in Ottawa, is doing his utmost to reconcile French-English differences and to save Confederation. Daniel, resentful of things as they are, holds his father's generation to blame and turns, irresponsibly and heatedly, to anarchy. MacLennan brings out, clearly and forcefully, good historical and sociological reasons for this agonising collision, and he shows Daniel, whom he pictures as being in many ways representative of the youth of the 1960's, to be a victim of circumstance. But MacLennan is at pains to point out the futility of rebellion for its own sake, as he refers often to the chastening experiences of

[127]

Alan's generation—the aftermath of the 1914-18 War, the Depression, the Spanish Civil War, and the Hitler War.

As seen here, the only answer—embodied by Alan—for Canada and, ultimately, the rest of the world, is patient and honourable statesmanship informed by an understanding of history. Yet the novel ends on a hopeless note with Daniel in jail for incipient terrorism and Alan, because of both his honest sympathy for Quebec and his son's antics, ousted by his fellow politicians.

The father-son dissension and the contemporary milieu of Ottawa and Montreal offer the potential for an invigorating book; but MacLennan, because of artistic flaws, some of which have debilitated his previous novels, falters once more; *Return of The Sphinx,* while in certain respects wholly worthy of admiration, is an imperfect work of fiction.

In the first place, the plot is not as concrete, not as muscular, as the above summary suggests. For Alan also has a daughter, Chantal, who falls in love with an older man, his best friend, Gabriel Fleury, a wise and cultured exile from France. Also, Daniel has an affair with an older woman, Marielle, the mother of his girl friend and an exile from Morocco. The romantic interludes provided by these duos are helpful, as shall be shown, in giving weight to the thematic context of the novel; however, they at the same time distract our attention from the main plot and contribute to the decidedly jerky movement of the narrative.

MacLennan has divided his three hundred pages into four sections. Book One covers one hundred and sixty-three pages; then comes an "Intermezzo" of thirty-two pages; then the eighty-eight pages of Book Two; and finally, a seven-page Epilogue.

Book One introduces us to all of the afore-mentioned characters and to most of the other figures in the novel: Alan's boss, Moses Bulstrode, a bullish, pragmatic, self-made politician; Herbert Tarnley, a wealthy businessman who is upset about his future prospects in a seething Quebec; Aimé Latendresse, Daniel's inspiration, an ex-priest of sour temperament fanatically devoted to the concept of an independent Quebec; and Joe Lacombe, an R.C.M.P. officer who served under Alan in the 1939-45 War and who, while still

Alan's close friend, is responsible for investigating the separatist activities of Daniel and Latendresse.

In these pages the backgrounds of the characters are dis-
closed to us and a flimsy sort of tension is built up. We
learn that Alan, because of his conscientious attachment to
his political beliefs, has not seen much of his children. He
is battling—in gentlemanly fashion—for a bilingual civil service. Bulstrode, while not convinced of the necessity of
Quebec's demands, stands by Ainslie. Meanwhile, Lacombe
breaks the news to Alan that Daniel has been a participant
in a Montreal riot and has become the moderator of a television programme in which he encourages Latendresse to
air his separatist views. At the same time the romances
flourish, and Book One ends with Alan driving home to
Montreal to see his son and daughter, only to find the family
apartment empty: Chantal is sleeping with Gabriel, Daniel
with Marielle.

The Intermezzo covers the next day, a Sunday. Alan drives
to his summer cottage north of Montreal in hopes of finding
his children there. Chantal and Daniel wake up in their
strange beds, she happily, he guiltily. Latendresse is seen
briefly as he enters a church, then leaves without taking the
Sacrament and returns to a book on bomb-building. Daniel
eventually heads for the cottage, but his car breaks down
on the way. Father and son fail to meet, and at the end of
the section Alan, back in Ottawa, has an inconclusive and
unhappy telephone conversation with Chantal, then turns
again to the political wars.

If we pause here, it should be possible to examine some
of the reasons why *Return of The Sphinx* is not a satisfying
work of art.

MacLennan is dealing with a set of interrelated conflicts—
Father against Son, Generation against Generation, Love
against Hate, Quebec against Canada, Alan against Parliament; these grating concussions are felt early in the novel,
and should, as the story progresses, build up like thunder in
the reader's consciousness. But the murmurs are heard with
only half an ear, and the impending storm is largely dissipated.

Too much attention is focused on Gabriel and Chantal,

especially in these first two hundred pages. Neither ever really stands out as a major character, yet we see at least as much of them as we do of Alan and Daniel. Gabriel's part is to supply information about Alan, to philosophise on a variety of matters, to bridge, with Chantal, through love, the generation gap, and to symbolise an uprooted and perishing civilisation of culture and manners. In his role of mentor he follows in the steps of Angus Murray, Captain Yardley, Matt McCunn, Dugald MacKenzie and Jerome Martell. But Gabriel, in spite of the wisdom he imparts, is bloodless and dull—almost unreal; an aging, sorrowful figure slowly shaking his head at the state of things and absent-mindedly stroking Chantal while he lets his memory range back over a cluttered past.

Chantal (who has much in common with other of MacLennan's females, notably Penny Wain, Lucy Cameron and Sally Martell) is a good deal more credible. Older than her brother, and estimably level-headed, she comes to Gabriel out of disgust with the hostile selfishness and antics of her own generation; but she at the same time exhibits genuine compassion and love-hunger and an engaging sense of her own inadequacies. And of course she gives us a number of insights where her family is concerned, but we discover eventually that her comments and thoughts about Alan and Daniel add little to our understanding of them. It is more important that we understand that she looks to the past for succour, that she finds the virtues that Gabriel represents (reason, a sense of duty, love of beauty, good manners) to be worth living with and preserving.

However, these virtues are also her father's, and although this fact makes for interesting psychological speculation, it also dilutes the impact which Alan, as the protagonist, should have upon the reader. Gabriel, bloodless or not, is a surrogate "hero," and his affairs do distract our attention from Alan and his predicament.

The relationship between Daniel and Marielle is not as much of an obstacle to the flow of the story as that between Gabriel and Chantal because Daniel is one of the two principal characters in the book, and this episode helps to bring us closer to him. Still, one senses an unnaturalness here: one feels that the author forces this union mainly in order to illuminate *his* generation's views—here is MacLennan's chance, as it were, to demonstrate to Daniel the futility of his radicalism. What we are given, then, in spite of Marielle's (unconvincing) declaration of love for the boy, is not so much a meeting of individuals as it is a clash of attitudes and ideas.

Marielle, motherly, kind-hearted and suitably sexy, is, as well, a voice of experience. She knows, as Daniel doesn't, that lust for independence can breed corruption, that political passions and ideals seldom make for a happier, better world, that human beings are limited creatures much given to selfishness; she knows that love is more valuable than hatred, that violent protest creates repression, and that war is hell. All this she tells Daniel, and she speaks from personal experience. She also speaks very much as a woman, and the gist of her views about life is this: "There is so little time to enjoy it, yet what else is it here for?" [1]

Daniel we have met before. He is Marius Tallard resuscitated; like Marius, he turns against his father; like Marius, he is sexually shackled by a Jansenist education (he shrinks with guilt following his first night with Marielle); like Marius, he is at odds with the other child in his family; like Marius, he thirsts for a free Quebec. MacLennan shows us that Daniel must be partly excused for his actions: his father has been too immersed in serving his country to give Daniel all the guidance and advice he needs; Quebec *has* been treated carelessly and with condescension by the rest of the country; Americanisation *is* a threat to the French-Canadian life-style; the world *has* been convulsed by one misery on top of another since the end of World War II; older people *have* been guilty of hypocrisy—at one point, Lacombe tells Alan:

"You see, Alan, these kids—a lot more of us than the kids, too—they've been really shocked by what those investigations turned up about graft and payola in *la belle province* only a few years ago. A lot of them suspect their fathers were taking it and they're right—a lot of their fathers were. They even think some priests were in on it. Well, you know how they'd all been taught to respect their elders and any kind of authority. . . . Well, it can be a pretty bad shock when a young fellow finds out that men he's been taught to respect are crooks or grafters or liars. . . ."[2]

Furthermore, MacLennan presents Daniel in such a way as to show that he is torn between love and respect for his father and allegiance to the separatist cause.

Be that as it may, Daniel fails to deeply engage one's sympathy. Given several opportunities to change his outlook, or to at least moderate it, he never does; he feels some sorrow at the prospect of deliberately sabotaging and humiliating his own father, but goes on to do so anyway. And although Daniel is, for most of the book, an unwilling tool of the terror-minded Latendresse, his shrill ranting, total lack of humour, and appalling indifference to history blot out most of the sorrow or pity we might otherwise feel for him.

Daniel is a credible, dynamic character—indeed, he will be familiar to most readers of this novel. They will have seen him screaming for the television cameras during a hundred riots; they will have seen him featured in the pages of *Life* and *Look* and the news magazines; they will have seen, heard, and read about him week in and week out since 1964. That is the trouble—Daniel, while not a hackneyed creation, comes across more as a representative of his generation of radicals than he does as a memorable individual. We know him, but only from a distance, for he is curiously one-dimensional. The few facts MacLennan gives us about Daniel's background seem detached, remote, from what he is and does. MacLennan skilfully exposes, mainly through dialogue, the surface emotions—and some of the inner turmoil—of this boy, but one never really becomes intimately acquainted with him. However, this portrayal of Daniel may be unhesitatingly accepted by many who themselves are unable to understand their own radicalised children, let alone the roots, motives, and emotional intricacies of the widespread youth rebellion.

Latendresse, who is clearly a far worse person than Daniel, makes an excellent villain. Embittered and self-righteously fanatical, he has become a glutton for political power and recognition because of his twisted, frustrated life. He is a seedy Hitler, and his divisive comments, dangerous insights regarding the psychological manipulation of audiences, and mad-dog personality make one all the more conscious of the value of Alan's aims.

When, after the first sixty pages of the story, we finally meet Alan Ainslie, we've already learned—from Tarnley, Gabriel, and Chantal—what to expect. Gabriel says that Alan "squirms" when people describe him as a Canadian nationalist: "Political nationalism is the last thing he'd go out for. He has a curious mystique about the country. He really loves it."[3] Tarnley remarks that Alan "is too naive for the profession of politics," and Gabriel thinks, "what kind of world would you be able to buy your way into, Mr. Tarnley, if there were no men in it like this one you call naive?"[4] Chantal regrets her father's idealistic service to an unthankful and unresponsive Canada, but Gabriel recalls how Alan once said to him, "That funny country I come from, if she can accept her own nature, and live with it, is going to become priceless to mankind."[5] Also in these and later pages we discover Alan to have been a merchant seaman; an Olympic athlete; a war hero (D.F.C. and one eye missing); a magazine editor whose publication folded under American competition; and a "clairvoyant" confidant of the Soviet ambassador to the U.N.—indeed, it is strongly suggested that Alan, while at the U.N., was instrumental in creating "such co-existence as there now was."

Then, when we see him fully revealed as a man of refinement, honour, and high ideals, but lonely, and self-tortured by the failure of his quest for personal happiness and Canadian harmony, our suspicions are confirmed: other men do look out of his sad eyes—Neil MacRae; Athanase and Paul Tallard; his stepfather, Daniel Ainslie; George Stewart and Jerome Martell. He shares his dream for Canada with Neil and Paul, his active youth with Neil, Paul and Jerome, his culture and high principles with Athanase and Daniel, his clairvoyance with Jerome; his being an orphan with Neil and Jerome; his feelings of defeat with Athanase, Daniel, and George, his loneliness with all of them.

But perhaps the most sensible way of relating Alan to other of MacLennan's characters is to remember how, at the

conclusion of *Two Solitudes,* Paul Tallard went forth to
World War II with faith in Canada's future. That is what
Alan did, too—but during the ensuing years he has come to
resemble, more and more, Paul's father, Athanase, a gentle-
man victimised by practical men of power, betrayed by a
son, his world, his hopes, and the standards he believes in
crumbling around him. Like Athanase Tallard, Alan Ainslie
is losing a battle with the times in which he lives; it is significant that a book he has written is given the title *Death of
a Victorian:* ". . . the Victorian who had died was himself.
This Victorian had been dying slowly for many years. . . ." [6]

Alan is a believable character, but only sporadically is he
a vital one. This fault can be attributed to two factors: we
are too seldom in contact with him—he makes his first
appearance in Chapter Five (page 64), and is at the centre
of our attention for only seventy-two of the first two hundred
and one pages of the book; secondly, he spends much time
roaming back to the past in thought and conversation, so
that his present affairs, urgent as they are, lack real immediacy.

Prior to Book Two Alan has three "live" conversations,
one of them of brief duration with Chantal over the telephone; the others are with Bulstrode and Joe Lacombe.

These two men (along with Chantal) may be the most
attractive characters in the novel. Bulstrode, an ex-circus
strongman from northern Ontario, speaks with vigour, puts
his faith in "the common sense of the ordinary citizen," stands
undaunted before the onslaughts of his political enemies,
exhibits a foursquare loyalty to Alan, and has a gift for
relating his ambitions and principles to the realm of the
possible instead of the ideal. Alan needs, and gets, his pro-
tection, and this fact in itself increases Bulstrode's stature in
our estimation. It is mostly those scenes containing Bulstrode
that bring to life for us, in a convincing way, the divisive
attitudes regarding the Quebec problem and the motivations
behind the attitudes.

Lacombe, like Gabriel, served under Alan during the war.
He is responsible for controlling subversive activities in Montreal, and is the first to break the news to Alan about Daniel's

participation in a separatist-inspired riot and about his sedi-
tious television show. Also, he encourages Alan to reminisce.
But Lacombe is not used by MacLennan merely as a con-
ductor between Alan and Daniel. It seems likely that he
symbolises the sort of Quebec MacLennan—and most
Canadians—would be comfortable with: a Quebec that retains
its individuality and pride but which also regards itself as a
responsible and integral part of a nation greater than itself.
Lacombe is a loyal and skilled R.C.M.P. officer, but he can
also tell Alan this:

> You know I've never had a damned thing myself against
> the English, but just the same I meant every word of what I
> just told you. *Ecoute, Alain*—this is where the difference is
> this time. In the old days, anyone who talked and felt the
> way I did left his people and went over to the English and
> disappeared among them. . . . This time that's not going to
> happen. This time we're staying *chez nous*. We want a
> *patrie,* and for the most of us Canada will do fine if the rest
> of you will ever get around to letting it become a *patrie* for
> all of us and not just for *les Anglais.*[7]

Lacombe, like Bulstrode, is made to seem important to the
reader because he is a man of action who protects and com-
forts the novel's hero.

Here it will be possible to enumerate the flaws of the first
two-thirds of this novel. It has been shown that the two love
affairs clot the flow of the story and contain built-in weaknesses of their own. In fact, the plot meanders sluggishly from
the very beginning, since the first chapter is given over to
Gabriel and a peripheral figure, the English-Canadian
businessman, Herbert Tarnley, and the second and third chapters mainly to Gabriel's recollections of his past. The plot,
then, is jumbled—the focus is switched with annoying fre-
quency from one set of characters to another.

Alan, Daniel and Gabriel, the leading characters, contain
deficiencies already noted, and second-level figures—Chantal,
Bulstrode and Lacombe—gather the better part of our esteem
and sense of identification. It is especially unfortunate that
the "old" men whom MacLennan holds up as paragons are so
lacking in fire, for their anemia thins the admiration we are

meant to feel for them. Also, there is a mob of peripheral characters who interfere with our concentration. Tarnley, although he does exemplify a type of person and an attitude that is enmeshed with the complexities of Quebec nationalism, fades off into the distant background after being made to seem important in Chapter One. Alan's dead wife and her prolific family are much discussed and thought of; although we need to know as much as possible about the background of the living Ainslies, MacLennan lavishes too much detail upon these recollections, and nearly builds up another, lesser, story. The same thing happens when Marielle remembers her father's death in the naval battle at Casablanca. Or when Gabriel recalls an English colonel with whom he escaped aboard ship from Singapore: the colonel is a wonderful caricature—the captain of the ship was jittery,

And when he sighted the ugly silhouette of a Japanese heavy cruiser against the sunset he changed course and ran for cover behind some small islands on his port bow. "Bloody fool!" was the colonel's comment on this. "The worst possible thing to do. Never turn tail to a tiger, a fighting pig or a native." [8]

—but MacLennan's ear for Blimpish speech-patterns only distracts us.

As has been implied, another digressive characteristic of the book is the tangle of flashbacks that it contains. These confuse and blur the immediacy of the action. We are made to visit, through ordinary flashbacks and metaphorical flights of imagination, Dauphiné, Avignon, Aix, French Indo-China, the Malacca Strait (aboard ship and in a lifeboat), Kenya, Morocco, the Caribbean (in a hurricane), England, Germany, the Yukon, Quebec City, Cape Breton, the Gaspé, the Olympic Games, a warplane, a commercial aircraft, and a glider. It is not too much to say that at times we don't know where we are.

So MacLennan unhesitatingly drifts off in all directions for two-thirds of the novel. Along the way one who follows him picks up an excellent variety of information about many events, ideas, and places—but perhaps it is not unfair to say that, in the process, one does not hesitate to put the book down from time to time.

Book Two, however, is much better. The afore-mentioned stylistic aimlessness is here transmogrified into a solid depiction of the results of the conflict between father and son. We see Bulstrode wrestling to save the power of his party—and Alan. Alan himself faces up to the disintegration of his political hopes and to the fact that his son has betrayed him, and Chantal and Daniel are brought into personal, bitter quarrel. In Chapter Four, perhaps the best-written section of the novel, Daniel and Alan come face to face for the first —and last—time; each hoping desperately for a reconciliation, but neither willing to sacrifice his beliefs, their exchange of dialogue reinforces our impressions of their temperaments in convincing fashion and moves us to pity, and to fully side with, Alan. This scene is itself reinforced by a slightly later clash between the two over the telephone. (Alan spends more time talking to his children over the telephone than he does face to face, and it may be that MacLennan has deliberately made this the case in order to suggest the physical uneasiness and "communication" difficulties that exist between "old" and young in our time; certainly these mechanised conversations sound authentic—they contain the awkward gaps, the unsatisfactory assumptions, the doubts, the things left unsaid, that are common to such exchanges.)

Daniel sinks further in our estimation—although we comprehend the reasons for his emotions—when he learns of the affair between Chantal and Gabriel and asks this gentle pair, "How can you be so disgusting?" By this time Alan has been destroyed in the House by furious reactions to a television collaboration between Latendresse and Daniel. Then Alan, returning to the Montreal apartment, finds Daniel and Marielle together in the bedroom he once shared with his wife. He drives his son out, and Daniel, frightened and suicidal, heads off at blazing speed in his car, carrying a bomb. He is captured by Lacombe, and Book Two comes to a satisfactorily disturbing finish:

"You know, Daniel, in my line of work I've met all kinds of them by this time. Most of them I can tell from their eyes and mouths and sometimes even by their ears, but the ones I always move first on I don't even have to look at." He put both hands on his stomach. "I don't have to look at them because I feel them right in here." Again he shook his head. "You know, Daniel, underneath you aren't any crazier than anyone else." And he added thoughfully, "That's what really scares me." [9]

At the end, Daniel fully exemplifies the frantic flailing out at authority that has been an everyday event of the 1960's. Lacombe's fright hits home, for Daniel, no gangster, had an education, a respectable background, and wanted, more than anything else, to find a cause, a new "religion," that would give meaning to his life.

Book Two contains, however, two minor things that might be objected to. First, Alan is momentarily brought together with an attractive spinster called Laura Sutherland, a complete newcomer to the story, and it is more or less implied that they'll eventually marry. Alan, to be sure, needs a woman's love, but this sudden, unexpected pairing is utterly irrelevant to the mainstream of the novel. The second point is this: Alan, for a reason which is not made clear, had never revealed the full story of his Cape Breton childhood to Daniel —the fact that he was an orphan, and that Archie MacNeil had killed his mother, etc. If MacLennan is indicating that Alan, like Neil MacRae and Jerome Martell, is seeking for himself and his country and the world the security and peaceful harmony that he never knew as a boy, this seems an awkward way of going about it. The intended link between this novel and *Each Man's Son* is, for all intents and purposes, non-existent—non-existent, but annoying, because one who has read the earlier book keeps puzzling over the matter. Also, there is a concomitant flaw: Daniel goes hunting through old newspapers for stories about his grandfather, and, for the first time, he begins to appreciate the continuum that is human history:

. . . Daniel was frightened. Those old newspapers had shaken him and now at last he knew what Uncle Gabriel meant when he said he had such a sense of *déjà vu*. Two world wars, more revolutions than he had ever heard of,

H-bombs and moon-shots and still people were saying, thinking and doing exactly the same things.[10]

One might expect that his attitude would be somewhat
changed by this lesson, but he no sooner is "shaken" than he
forgets what he has learned and heads toward his final
rampage.

Still, Book Two does harden the narrative; the protagonists
are at last brought to, and kept at, the centre of our attention;
their anguish becomes ours; and the climax, which is redolent
of the tortured 1960's, has a memorable impact.

Unfortunately, the novel does not end here. There is a
denouement which brings to mind the unnecessary last chapter
of *Two Solitudes*. Alan, stunned by all that has happened,
goes on a cross-country tour of Canada. When he returns to
his Laurentian cottage, he is refreshed by the presence of his
warm, simple country neighbours and by

Images of the land: the long wash of the decisive ocean
against the granite; sunlight spangling the mist over the
estuary the old navigator had mistaken for the Northwest
Passage leading to the indispensable dream; the prairie wind
almost as visible above the wheat as ruffling through it; the
antlers of a bull elk cascading down the side of a Rocky
Mountain; arrows of wild geese shooting off into the twilight
over the delta of the Athabasca . . .[11]

At the finish, Alan recognises the love he feels for both
his children, and for this land, "Too vast even for fools to
ruin all of it." He thanks God for saving Daniel, and the
final paragraph of the book echoes the conclusion of *The
Watch That Ends the Night*:

Looking over the lake he at last accepted that he had
merely happened into all this. Constance, Chantal, Daniel,
Gabriel—they and all the others had merely happened into
this loveliness that nobody could understand or possess, and
that some tried to control or destroy just because they were
unable to possess or understand it. Merely happened into
this joy and pain and movement of limbs, of hope, fear, shame
and the rest of it, the little chipmunk triumphs and defeats.
He believed it would endure. He thanked God he had been
of it, was of it.

Hugh MacLennan gives expression in this Epilogue to emotions and beliefs which move us to admiration. But admirable as these sentiments are, they are not art. There is here, as at the end of *Two Solitudes,* a failure of craftsmanship, of structure, of proportion. The atmosphere of loneliness, frustration, fear, and social futility that pervades the narrative awakens in the reader a sense of recognition and some degree of involvement. This incisive commitment to the book is at least partly dissolved by the soothing notions of the Epilogue.

Return of the Sphinx, like all of MacLennan's novels, is built around its themes. The title of the novel implies the central theme—what I have already described as "the unchanging capacity of men to do themselves—and their world —lasting injury." (The obvious relationship with Yeats's poem, "The Second Coming," needn't, I think, be elaborated upon.) What is important to an understanding of MacLennan's treatment of this theme is his explanation of the reasons for contemporary unrest and hopelessness:

I believe that the real cause of the world crisis—for that is what it is—no more respects frontiers than an influenza epidemic respects them. I believe the crisis came when humanity lost its faith in man's ability to improve his own nature. . . . When people no longer can believe in personal immortality, when society at large has abandoned philosophy, many men grow desperate without knowing why. They crack up—and don't know they have. Some of them will do *anything*—no matter how hopeless, criminal or idiotic— merely to have people mention their names and recognise that they exist. . . . A senseless crime can be one way of passing into the only kind of immortality this sick epoch understands, and so can the leadership of a senseless revolt —it can go onto the records and into the archives.[12]

This insight is applied in specific fashion to Daniel's ambitions:

Now he knew he had to liberate this nation even if it involved his own death. He heard his name mentioned with reverence by thankful people long after he was gone, as the Christians spoke the names of their martyrs. He heard the Jesuit speaking to little boys in the seminary: "Once he sat here just as you are sitting here now. Even then his face revealed his dedication. . . ."[13]

And Latendresse has been created as a "spoiled priest."

MacLennan brings into play against this false religion two thematic antidotes, the first of which is Love. Alan, Daniel, Chantal, Marielle, Gabriel, Laura Sutherland—all hunger for love, all need to share themselves with another human being; they know (Daniel perhaps instinctively) that only by doing so can they come to terms with themselves and a chaotic world. MacLennan stresses that the respect and compassion of family love is as integral a part of valuable life as the caring that exists between man and woman.

The other antidote is a unified and happy Canada. Early in the story, Gabriel remembers how Alan, while in a German prison camp, "had spoken of Canada in a homesick way full of a curious mixture of longing and deprecation. He wanted it to be so much more than it was." Later, Alan says to Daniel: "If Canada can hold together, she could become a pilot plant for a new kind of nation and a new kind of freedom and I'm not exaggerating the importance of that for the whole world. If two old cultures like the French and English can't work together within a single national home without destroying each other, what chance have all the others got in what has practically become a single world society?" [14]

Canada's future role as a model country is made to seem all the more indispensable by the author, since he, to all appearances, regards Europe as decadent and worn out and the United States as a juggernaut motored by uncontrollable megalomania.

It is Gabriel who seems to underline MacLennan's feelings about Europe:

It was on the second day home that he had begun meeting relations and old friends and at first they had all shocked him, they had seemed so old and scarred by their lives. He heard them saying the same old things and realised that in spite of the war they had been doing the same old things. [15]

Far more information is supplied about the American stranglehold on Canada and much of the rest of the world. Alan's magazine failed because "it had no chance against the American competition and control of the advertising market." Tarnley admits "that ever since the war Canadian businessmen have been getting rich by quietly selling out this country's future for capital gains to American interests." Ainslie, describing a conversation overheard on a plane from New York to Montreal, likens American businessmen to "tax farmers in the Roman Empire:"

"This particular set of them had bottles and they were talking as though this was a charter flight and they owned the whole plane for the evening. I heard one of them say— . . . 'These boobs up here will do anything you ask them to. All you have to do is wave a contract in their kissers and they'll sign it without even reading the fine print.' . . . Then another said, 'This is better than South America ever knew how to be, and these are nice people up here. Real nice.' Then another of them said, 'That you can say again. Real nice people.' Then they all laughed together and then, Joe, I got mad." [16]

Bulstrode dislikes "this P.R. image stuff that's come in from the States." Chantal explains that the Ainslies were a happy family—it was only "when we went to New York that everything changed." Daniel tells us that "In Asia the Americans are bombing and burning alive helpless people—and for what? They tell us exactly for what—to compel those people to sit docile while the Americans pour in money and equipment to destroy the ancient Asian cultures and turn them into the culture of Coca-Cola and the supermarket." And he also gives vent to this explosion:

In the old days, the empires went after slaves and raw materials, but now what the Americans are after is consumers. That's their famous Way of Life—turn the whole world into consumers of American products. If they keep on getting away with it, it will mean they've turned the whole world into a colossal American supermarket with cheap copies of Americans in there, buying, . . . They've taken over the English in this country completely, and now they're after us. Those products they sell here—do you know the way they do it? They hire French Canadians to go down to the States to translate their advertising slogans into French. That's their idea of culture—advertising.[17]

But MacLennan's disgust with the U.S.A. is, by the time of this novel, part of his larger disenchantment with the modern cheapening of the quality of our lives. He finds time to strike at mass communications; universities; mindless destruction of valuable landmarks and older dwellings to make way for sterile high-rise structures of steel, concrete and glass; polluted air; the volume of urban noise; dress styles among the young; the decay of religion; commercial ugliness ("Now the night through which he drove was harsh . . . where the neon signs smouldered over barbecues and filling stations and headlights stabbed and tires rushed and screamed. . . ."); the replacement of the genuine by the artificial in the guise of processed cheese—cheese that is scientifically treated "to look cheesier than real cheese;" time-payment plans; the forced aging of the young ("The youth of the world was over. The world's youth was made middle aged before it had grown up. There was no comfort left for the youth of the world. They had taken it away. The System had taken it away."); North American rootlessness, caused by the new mobility as "families are shunted from place to place in government and the corporations."

At the same time, MacLennan realises that these disturbing phenomena are, like the discord between generations, symptoms of a larger danger:

The time he was living in was too fantastic for anyone to look it square in the eye. Hurricane weather but no hurricanes. Nuclear confrontations with serious-minded men seriously wondering whether there would be even a blade of grass left on the planet inside a few years, but so far no bombs. Full employment but no security. Knowledge in unknowable quantities but never so many people telling each other they could not understand. All the ideas that had guided and inspired Ainslie's life—socialism, education, the faith that science and prosperity would improve man's life, even the new psychology which everyone so glibly talked—the best he could say now of any of these hopes was that they had foundered in the ancient ocean of human nature.[18]

MacLennan, then, is desperately worried and saddened by the diseases of our time, and in this book he gives expression to these matters which concern us all. Although there is heavy emphasis on the themes, they are skilfully interwoven and are all-important to an appreciation of the novel. But because of the weight given these related topics, because MacLennan is so obviously *convinced* that the world is going from bad to worse and is taking Canada along with it, the Epilogue is seen to be all the more a weak, useless appendage to the novel. MacLennan spends nearly three hundred pages telling us that the future, ripped by hatreds or benumbed by homogenisation, will not be worth living for. Then he turns around and tells us that life is beautiful.

Once more this man has failed to "create a whole which is harmonious;" once more his appetite for ideas interferes with his obligations as a novelist. There occur, again, examples of stilted dialogue, unnatural revelations of thought-processes, and careless use of figurative language. Again we are presented with characters who are a bit too familiar.

Nonetheless, uneven as it is, *Return of The Sphinx* is a powerful book. The conflicts, because they are of such moment, demand the reader's concern, and they, along with the facts which cause them, make an impression which is not easily forgotten. MacLennan might also say of this novel, as he did of *Two Solitudes,* that "it happened to put into words what hundreds of thousands of Canadians felt and knew." And not only Canadians.

CHAPTER EIGHT

∼ CONCLUSION

IT WAS SUGGESTED in the introduction that Hugh MacLennan's main flaws as a novelist result from his using techniques which properly belong to non-fiction and from what must be called poverty of the imagination. Having examined the novels, it will now be possible to evaluate the validity of this double charge.

Because MacLennan is primarily concerned with instructing his readers he employs, time and time again, a style which belongs to the essayist or the pamphleteer. One noticed the beginnings of this trend in *Barometer Rising*—the long, unassimilated comments on the history and the sociological background of Halifax and Canada. MacLennan's method of purveying these observations to us was, to say the least, clumsy: he pumped his characters full of the necessary information and gradually squeezed it out of them from first chapter to last; sometimes the material flowed frozen from the brain, sometimes from the mouth. One was uncomfortably aware that one was being lectured, one knew that the major characters were puppets, and that the strings connecting them with the author were wired for sound. This unfortunate blunder also flawed the second half of *Two Solitudes* and all of *The Precipice*. But MacLennan has not been willing to entirely trust his characters with his tenets—he himself must break in occasionally to back them up; we saw the most flagrant examples of this artistic neuroticism in the last chapter of *Two Solitudes,* in the introduction to *The Precipice,* and in the "Author's Note" and the beginning of the twenty-third chapter of *Each Man's Son.* What happens is that the author, instead of remaining at a comfortable distance from us, comes, grimly determined, stamping into view: Hugh MacLennan, novelist, is transmogrified into Sergeant-Major MacLennan.

The second crippling factor, poverty of imagination, can most easily be understood by glancing at the cast of characters. One need only compare the cast of *Barometer Rising* with those of the later novels; the future figures are slightly different, to be sure; but the basic characters who first appeared in *Barometer Rising* are still recognisable.

Penelope Wain becomes Heather Methuen, then Lucy Cameron, Margaret Ainslie, and Catherine; each is mature, wholesomely attractive, independent by nature, loyal to her man, and intelligent; also, except for Margaret, each breaks with a social background which she feels to be stultifying. Even Sally Martell and Chantal Ainslie, younger though they be, share most of these traits. Then there is the termagant: Aunt Maria Wain, Janet Methuen, Jane Cameron, George's Aunt Agnes. Each of these older women is domineering, and each, significantly, is loyal to a rigidly classified society, to notions of social conformity, and to Great Britain. Angus Murray, Yardley, Matt McCunn, Dugald MacKenzie, and, to a considerable extent, Jerome Martell, can each be called a sage, or the "conscience" of their novels. This man is older than the hero and his counsel to him or to the heroine is invariably of great value; he has white or grey hair and is rough-tongued but beneficent. (Gabriel Fleury has dark hair, is soft-spoken, and his wise remarks achieve little because of the thematic nature of *Return of The Sphinx,* but he is still recognisable a sage.) Usually the antagonist, or villain, is a corrupting influence, a businessman out for all he can get, insensitive, ruthless and hard—Geoffrey Wain, Huntly McQueen, Carl Bratian, Herbert Tarnley; Sam Downey, although he has a minor role, also fits this category. MacLennan's heroes are also types. They share similar fates; each undergoes a great ordeal from which he is rescued at the last minute (the sole exceptions being Athanase Tallard and the sub-hero, Archie MacNeil); in all of the novels but the last this event coincides with a union of the hero and his wife. But even in *Return of The Sphinx,* Laura Sutherland would seem

to be waiting for Alan. The ordeal involves separation between lovers as well as a grappling with whatever problem
is on the MacLennan agenda. Neil MacRae, Athanase and
Paul Tallard, Stephen Lassiter, Daniel Ainslie, Archie Mac-
Neill, George Stewart, and Alan Ainslie are all tortured by
self-doubt, and all of them are humourless and singularly
unlikeable. (Archie and Alan are perhaps less unlikeable than
the rest.) Jerome Martell only emphasises this mirror-effect,
for he can be seen as a composite of earlier characters. Like
Neil MacRae, he has suffered in war and like him he returns
to the woman he loves; he is a brilliant medical man like
Daniel Ainslie, and a counsellor of more than Dugald Mac-
Kenzie's calibre; his physical prowess and attraction for
women is reminiscent of Stephen Lassiter; like Paul Tallard,
he is a former athlete going grey at the temples; practically
the only new thing about him is his evangelical zeal. It might
also be noted that four of the leading figures in the books are
doctors—Murray, Ainslie, MacKenzie and Martell. The
marked similarity between Marius Tallard and Daniel Ainslie
II should not escape our attention, either.

We will see further, as we progress, how MacLennan's
weak imagination and obsession with theme affect various
aspects of the novels.

Characterisation undoubtedly suffers most. As already
noted, the major characters are inevitably torch-bearers for
whatever idea MacLennan happens to think important at the
time. Only in the first half of *Two Solitudes* and in *Each
Man's Son,* and in a less perfect way in *Return of The Sphinx,*
does MacLennan manage successfully to fuse his characters
with his theme. In creating Athanase Tallard, MacLennan
had to make an effort at using his imagination because he
himself was not French; and the first half of this book
illustrates an imaginative capability that has otherwise lain
dormant. In *Each Man's Son* MacLennan did not really have
to exercise his imagination, because he was writing out of
cultural and environmental awareness; in spite of the weight
of emphasis on Calvinism, the story and its characters ring
true.

Elsewhere, what is the strength of *Each Man's Son* contributes to the over-all debility. Neil MacRae, Paul Tallard,

Lucy Cameron, George Stewart and Alan Ainslie, as well as the respective "sages" and a number of peripheral characters, are all, in a sense, Hugh MacLennan—instead of themselves. MacLennan refuses, or is unable (with some minor exceptions) to give them a life of their own; they are essentially vehicles for the theme. Neil and Murray tell us about Canadian identity, reflecting MacLennan's new-found realisation of the same; Paul Tallard is a shell stuffed with notes about writing "Canadian" novels; Lucy gives us MacLennan's confusing opinions of the differences between Canadians and Americans; George Stewart and Martell reflect, in an over-emotional and unconvincing way, a personal trial through which the author had previously passed; and Alan Ainslie exhibits MacLennan's opinions and feelings with respect to the chaotic state of modern man and society. Instead of writing out of his imagination, then, MacLennan has written out of personal experience and personal agonisings. He does not *create* characters; he sketches a picture of someone whose appearance, or even whose sex, may not be his own, but who is, when you come right down to it, demonstrably a version of himself—a different body with MacLennan's brain and thoughts.

The characters, and of course the novels themselves, suffer also from grave deficiencies of style. Plots tend to be turgid stereotypes; that is, the general framework of them is that of the typical romance. Hero and heroine are joined on the last page and walk, as it were, hand in hand, backs to us, off into the sunset. But even here there is a sub-crippling effect. These hazy finales have about them an indecisiveness; unsatisfactory in themselves, they also leave a loose end to the novel. One is never sure that things are really going to be all that much better in the future—what *is* life going to be like for Neil, Paul, Stephen, Ainslie, George, Alan and their women? Each of these protagonists has been so embittered, so trapped in thematic difficulties right to the end when he sees the light, and, to boot, so unadmirable, that one has a hard time to fancy them changing much. This factor goes back to characterisation, of course, but it is important to consider when evaluating plot.

Coupled with these bromidic plots is a weakness for commonplace sentimental distortion. This is evident in the love-scenes, where we find the hero, be it Stephen, Paul or George, professing his love in the inadequate clichés of hundreds of second-rate movies, novels, and magazine stories. MacLennan, despite his incessant lecturing about the evils of puritanism/Calvinism has himself apparently been unable to shake off youthful constraints. That he would presumably deny this allegation is shown by the following justification of his handling of sex in his novels:

The fact that the human body was kept out of love by the Victorians seems an inadequate reason for keeping the human soul out of it today. Yet it is a fact that in novel after novel the act of love is treated like the description of a problem in mechanical engineering. My heart sinks when I read through a long narrative dealing with the lives of lawyers or business men and come to the inevitable breaks, like the breaks for the television commercial, in which the hero goes to bed with the wife of his best friend and neither gets any fun out of it. I know perfectly well that this sort of thing causes a good many thousands of morons and deprived people to buy books they otherwise would not buy, but I still believe it is a passing fashion.[1]

One can sympathise with his attitude, but this does not compensate for the sort of love-scenes he does write. And it would be hard, indeed, to show where he himself has been really successful in portraying the "human soul." Certainly lasting affection is admirable and is a happy characteristic of MacLennan's views; but in the realistic novel, sex, if treated, should be treated believably. One grows tired of having MacLennan slam the bedroom door in one's face every time two people get close to one another; it is stiltedly old-fashioned, it does not help the novel in any way, and it detracts from our insight into the characters themselves.

Our insight where characters' motives are concerned is also limited by a generally awkward handling of internal revelation. The trouble here stems from MacLennan's prompting his puppets from off-stage, and it is most noticeable in the first three novels. But even as late as *The Watch That Ends the Night* we discover the same fault; here, it occurs as a result of what may be termed uncontrolled, hothouse-like

emotion. George's thoughts particularly contain a grandiloquence of phrasing that cannot be satisfactorily reconciled
with his characteristically mute ineffectiveness.

Also, thematic, sentimental, and too high-flown word
sequences take away from the validity of the dialogue. Jerome's guru-ish speeches are no less easy to believe in than
are Neil's manifestoes on Canadianism. One finds no originality or fire in the spoken word of these major figures; all are
terribly sincere, and speak exactly like one another. Paul
Tallard sounds like George Stewart and George sounds like
Neil MacRae who sounds like Lassiter or Daniel Ainslie or
Alan Ainslie. (Athanase Tallard, with his French inflection,
escapes this censure.) Likewise, the tedious, one-dimensional
"wisdom" and suffering patience of the heroines, as reflected
in their conversations, makes them interchangeable.

All of the above flaws become the more glaring when one
turns to examine MacLennan's minor characters, for they are
much more memorable than the major figures. The answer
to this paradox would seem to be that MacLennan, in
portraying these characters, was writing about people, or
"types," whom he had known instead of about himself. He
actually has a good ear for regional dialect and for intonation,
although one would never guess this from listening to his
protagonists. Maria Wain's snooty flair for self-assertion; the
seething frustrated anger of Marius Tallard and the young
Daniel Ainslie; Matt McCunn's priggish snorting; Angus the
Barraman's sibilant drunkenness; Dr. Bigbee's preposterous
Englishry—all ring with life; here, one feels, are real people,
individuals, speaking believably and colourfully.

Concomitantly, we find that MacLennan has an eye and
an ear for humour, and an engaging sense of the bizarre. One
remembers Matt McCunn telling his stolid niece, Lucy, how
he had a testicle shot off in the war, or Bill Blackett, the
hospitalised Newfoundlander in *Each Man's Son,* relating his
adventures to a wide-eyed Alan: "I knowed a girl in Dominica
oncet told me I 'ad the longest 'un she ever did see." [2] Mac-
Lennan's picture of Dr. Bigbee holed up with his paraphernalia
in Waterloo School not only serves the author's satiric
purpose, but is very funny as well—as is the sketch of the
English colonel in *Return of The Sphinx.*

These minor characters are vivid also because of artistic omission—they seldom have to think, are not victimised by the author's awkward rendering of internal revelation; speaking and acting, they engage the reader's interest and emotions. Also, most of them have a contribution to make to the theme of their novels. The termagants, as has been seen, are held up to ridicule for their straitlaced, reactionary attitudes; likewise, to take only two examples, Dr. Bigbee and Carl Bratian serve to underline what MacLennan considers to be the idiocies of the British and American influences. Big Alec MacKenzie of *Barometer Rising* is drawn with compassion and insight; through him, MacLennan laments the passing of old-time independence and craftsmanship in Cape Breton. One wishes that MacLennan would write a novel about *these* people, a novel about human beings instead of walking ideologies.

Background or setting, is also a strong point in MacLennan's fiction. If we are going to see any brilliance of style, we should, according to a number of MacLennan's critics, see it here. It can be argued, however, that MacLennan's settings are not extraordinarily well-done; that there is little evidence of a personal style; and that perhaps the scenes stand out principally because the protagonists are so uninteresting. It has been suggested earlier that familiarity may play a major part in the applause given MacLennan's pictures of Canada: in comparison with London, say, or California, very little has been written about Montreal or Nova Scotia, and Canadians are naturally pleased to come across descriptions of places which they know at first hand. Let us look at the following piece of description:

. . . we stepped outside and there from the front of the Arts Building was downtown Montreal like a fleet at anchor in an arctic port with all its lights on and the smoke going straight up. The campus was dark with its elm fountains lean and bare, but long rhomboids of light from the library windows fell across the snow and I saw students passing through them with their breath puffing out and heard their heels creaking on the packed snow. This campus was an island of quiet in the city's roar, and at night it was an island of dark in the city's blaze, and on this particular night it felt very cold.[3]

This is, beyond doubt, one of MacLennan's finest pieces of straight descriptive writing. The nautical simile is well-chosen, as is the one for the trees; the word "creaking" fits the time and place perfectly, and "rhomboids" lends a nice sense of the exact to the snapshot: one can see, in the mind's eye, the city spread out below, one can sense the cold and the hunched movement across the campus, one can hear the snow crunching underfoot and feel the cold in one's nostrils. In earlier chapters we took note of similar descriptions, and the same observations hold true here: a sparing use of figurative language set in sentences of ordinary length; but an ability to appeal to one's senses through lucid, straightforward phraseology is seen to be MacLennan's forte—clear, unoriginal writing.

Sometimes this gift for description is combined with a flair for historical imagination, as in the pictures of Halifax, or, as here, in George's description of Newcastle, New Brunswick:

These semi-ghost towns of a colonial past—we have several of them in that part of the country, and when you see them now it is hard to believe that once upon a time British officers in swallow-tail coats stepped ashore onto their wooden jetties from corvettes, frigates, and sloops-of-war. I remember the town's main street was a hundred yards of battered macadam containing two wooden churches, half a dozen shops, a sad red brick bank, a sadder red brick post-office with a four-faced clock on the roof. I can't remember the street's name, but I would lay even money it was either Wellington Street or King Street. . . . The only thing that seemed to matter in that town, except for the sawmills, was the railway station.[4]

Again, this is good visual description and does show a sense of historical awareness. But as a picture it is surely not exceptional, is, in fact, not as good as many descriptions of a similar nature by Thomas Raddall.

There is one type of description at which MacLennan does excel, however—"action-shots." To this writer, the two finest pieces of sustained writing in all the novels are those of the Halifax Explosion and its aftermath and of Archie MacNeill's last fight; here are brief excerpts from the latter:

He snapped a left into his face and liked the feel of its impact, but immediately Miller went into a crouch with nothing showing but arms, elbows, gloves, and the top of his head. Archie crossed his right and felt a stab of pain and wondered if he had broken a knuckle on Miller's skull. He slammed another right into the pork-barrel body and felt pain again. . . . He decided to work over Miller methodically, but the pork-barrel body exploded against him and his head snapped back in a cloud of stars as Miller butted in the clinch. Archie felt ashamed to be caught by a butt in the first round, shook loose and went after Miller in a rage. He found nothing but arms and elbows and he seemed to have been punching for hours before the gong ended the round.[5]

Archie stepped back with trembling knees and a white coldness clamping his forehead and knew he was through. Miller rolled heavily on the floor and got his elbows under his chest. . . . He swung his right and it landed feebly on Miller's hulking shoulders. Then Miller bent down like a crab, lurched around, grabbed Archie by the waist and hung on. By the time the clinch was broken, he was at least as fresh as Archie was. The round petered out in fumbles and clinches and Archie's legs were weaving when he went back to his corner.[6]

Clearly, MacLennan knows his boxing: one is in the ring with MacNeill, one feels his momentary exultation, his pain, his overpowering weariness. Simply contrast the power of this prose with the self-conscious, fuzzy dogmatism of one of George's reminiscences and it can be readily seen how uneven MacLennan's prose style is:

In the Thirties old John Donne had spoken for all of us when he declared that no man is an island entire in itself, that every man is a piece of the continent, a part of the main. In the bleak years we at least were not alone. In these prosperous years we were. The gods, false or true, had vanished. The bell which only a few years ago had tolled for all, now tolled for each family in its prosperous solitude. So with us; so with so many. How private my life with Catherine had become! How outmoded so many of my friends felt! How different was this new key![7]

Should MacLennan ever write a novel in which he combined real people with action-packed events, he would be bound to increase his stature as a craftsman; he came close to success on these terms in *Each Man's Son*. But as of this date, his artistry suffers badly from a vapid or overly emotional insistence upon ideas, and from a crippling want of originality. With the partial exceptions already mentioned, MacLennan's novels are, apparently for himself and certainly for the reader, not so much art as heavy labour.

This leads one to try to determine MacLennan's views about individual man. It would seem, if we go by the Mac-Lennan hero, that life is a desperate battle, a vale of tears from which one can wrest semi-contentment only through coming to terms with some overwhelmingly important ideology and through the devotion of a loyal woman who understands, and sympathises with, one's problems. In such a person's life there would be little or no room for humour, and love relationships would be dedicated, soft, and semi-mystical. Sexual union with one's lover would cease while one agonised over the enormity of the current problem—be it Canada's coming-of-age, learning to be a novelist, disgruntlement with one's profession, a soul-searching analysis of repressions suffered in childhood, spiritual weakness and a guilt complex for one's own generation, or the present state of the world. Salvation would arise for the man only with full "self-knowledge;" the woman would stand by through these trials of time, a faithful and discerning partner waiting, as it were, at the end of the tunnel. Conventional religion would be virtually discarded, but one would never cease to be grateful for the wonder and the beauty of life. There may be further severe trials in the future, but *somewhere* ahead there is reason for hope. One would do well, would save one's soul almost, by going into medicine instead of business.

But almost certainly this view is true only in part. The sort of person who emerges above is the end-product of Mac-Lennan's artistic weakness, and not a predetermined Everyman. However, what are, for MacLennan, desirable human qualities stand out: one should be faithful in one's human relationships, and one should be concerned about one's own world—one must not turn his back on the rigours of life, but must constantly strive to better himself and those parts of life he touches. This twofold philosophy of faithfulness and valuable ambition is not remarkable in itself, but it is unusual in this era, the heyday of the anti-hero. It is a pity that the virtues inherent in such a belief are not put across better in the novels.

We have determined that a main prerequisite for MacLennan's Everyman is that he must shake off all constraining influences of environment and history. And this brings one to MacLennan's opinions of Canada. Very much a Canadian nationalist, he is a fervid opponent of the British influence: witness the attacks on Geoffrey Wain, the Loyalist legacy in Grenville, or Montreal-English high society. While ridding ourselves of all vestiges of the Anglo-Saxon oppressor, we must do our utmost to unify French-and English-speaking Canada. In unshackling our guilt complexes, the result of Calvinism, we will at last live up to our capabilities. But we must not be governed by the materialistic lust of the Americans. It is interesting to note, after examining the six novels, that Canada itself is seen as an innocent being raped by outsiders: Europeans were guilty for the 1914-18 War, along with pseudo-"Europeans" like Geoffrey Wain; the British aura is a divisive factor in French-English relationships; "American" Puritanism is a deadly menace, and "Canadian" Calvinism is just as dangerous—but it derives from Scotland; Sam Downey, the American fight-manager is evil, but the French-Canadian fight-manager befriends Archie. If at times one wearies, especially of MacLennan's ranting against the Anglo-Saxons, one still recognises his fairness, for he goes out of his way to attack his Scottish inheritance of a fearsome religion, and illustrates, too, the stultifying conformities of Roman Catholic dogma. Nonetheless, a clear picture of the Canada MacLennan desires never emerges. He wants progress, but not on American terms; yet he never answers the question of how Canadians are to retain individuality as a nation if they cast off all the tradition which has set them apart from the United States for so long.

But, finally, MacLennan's faults of insight and craftsmanship must not blind one to the nature of his lasting achievement. To read, in chronological succession, all of MacLennan's novels is to see how this man who loves Canada has himself made an Odyssey. The Neil MacRae who headed inland from Halifax with earnest optimism was also Hugh MacLennan, and it is only now, in the late days of the 1960's, five novels later, that the high hopes with which he set out are seen to have been overwhelmed by an indifferent reality. The world has come to Canada at last, and the innocence and potential with which MacLennan invested this country has, in the long run, proved illusory. *Return of The Sphinx* brings MacLennan to the end of his long quest, but the landfall is no fortunate one. For Alan Ainslie's affliction is also Hugh MacLennan's; the two are nearly indistinguishable—far from Cape Breton now, they have both seen their unselfish energies dissipated, their dreams vanquished.

Nevertheless, the all-important thing is that MacLennan made this voyage into the previously uncharted waters of a nation's spirit and being. The challenge he met was of his own making, but all the more worthwhile for that. Reading his novels, his explorations, one cannot help but admire his determination and courage, his sincerity of purpose, his dedication to his land. Years ago, he said:

One of the reasons why we write books is because we are lonely, and another is that we want to come to terms with our environment by telling the truth about it. These two desires are in perpetual conflict in any writer who ever lived. He has to choose between them and to choose is painful.[8]

Hugh MacLennan has come to terms with Canada more fully and in some ways more memorably than any other writer. His achievement in this respect is in a class by itself, and his novels are sure to stand for a very long time as landmarks of the Canadian experience.

～ NOTES

Chapter I

1. Ian Grimble, *The Trial of Patrick Sellar*, London, Routledge & Kegan Paul, 1962, p. xiii.
2. *Ibid.*
3. Hugh MacLennan, *Scotchman's Return and Other Essays*, Toronto, MacMillan Co. of Canada Ltd., 1960, p. 8.
4. *Ibid.*, p. 64.
5. Hugh MacLennan, *Cross-Country*, Toronto, Collins, 1949, p. 26.
6. *Ibid.*, p. 27.
7. *Ibid.*, p. 103.
8. Hugh MacLennan, *Thirty and Three*, ed. Dorothy Duncan, London, MacMillan & Co. Ltd., 1955, pp. 13-15.
9. Letter to writer, 30 July, 1965.
10. *Thirty and Three*, p. 20.
11. Letter to writer.
12. *Ibid.*
13. *Thirty and Three*, pp. 80-81.
14. *Cross-Country*, p. 39.
15. *Ibid.*, pp. 40-41.
16. *Ibid.*, pp. 44-45.
17. *Ibid.*, p. 45.
18. *Thirty and Three*, p. 165.
19. *Scotchman's Return*, p. 239.
20. *Cross-Country*, p. 46.
21. *Ibid.*, p. 49.
22. *Ibid.*, p. 51.
23. *Scotchman's Return*, pp. 275-276.
24. *Ibid.*, p. 10.
25. *Cross-Country*, p. 44.
26. Letter to writer.
27. *Scotchman's Return*, p. 16.
28. *Thirty and Three*, p. 134.
29. George Woodcock, "A Nation's Odyssey: The Novels of Hugh MacLennan," *Masks of Fiction*, ed. A.J.M. Smith, Canada, McClelland and Stewart Ltd., New Canadian Library, 1961, p. 129.
30. *Ibid.*, p. 131.
31. *Thirty and Three*, p. 249.
32. *Scotchman's Return*, p. 219-220.
33. *Cross-Country*, p. 50.
34. Letter to George Barratt, 5 March, 1935.
35. *Cross-Country*, p. 52.
36. Letter to George Barratt, 20 October, 1941.
37. Woodcock, p. 129.
38. *Cross-Country*, p. 159.
39. Letter to Barratt, 1941.
40. *Scotchman's Return*, p. 244.
41. *Ibid.*, p. 149.
42. *Ibid.*, p. 153.
43. *Ibid.*, pp. 155-156.
44. *Ibid.*, p. 157.
45. *Ibid.*, p. 158.
46. *Ibid.*, p. 145.
47. *Ibid.*, p. 147.

Chapter II

1. *Thirty and Three*, p. 52.
2. Hugh MacLennan, *Barometer Rising*, Toronto, MacMillan Co. of Canada Ltd., St. Martin's Classics, 1948, p. 5.
3. *Ibid.*, p. 6.
4. *Ibid.*, p. 14.
5. *Ibid.*, p. 229.
6. *Ibid.*, pp. 247-248.
7. *Ibid.*, pp. 9-10.
8. *Ibid.*, p. 75.
9. *Ibid.*, p. 232.
10. *Ibid.*, p. 154.
11. *Ibid.*, p. 111.
12. *Ibid.*, p. 37.
13. *Ibid.*, pp. 131-132.

14. *Ibid.*, p. 55.
15. *Ibid.*, p. 212.
16. *Ibid.*, pp. 329-330.
17. *Ibid.*, p. 343.
18. *Ibid.*, pp. 358-359.
19. Edmund Wilson, *O Canada*, New York, Farrar, Staus & Giroux, 1965, p. 78.
20. M.H. Abrams, *A Glossary of Literary Terms*, New York, Holt, Rinehart and Winston, 1960, pp. 2-3.
21. *Thirty and Three*, p. 53.
22. Abrams, p. 101.
23. *Thirty and Three*, p. 53.

Chapter III

1. Wilson, p. 100.
2. *Scotchman's Return*, p. 266.
3. Hugh MacLennan, *Two Solitudes*, New York, Duell, Sloan and Pearce, 1945, p. 8.
4. *Ibid.*, p. 116.
5. *Ibid.*, p. 196.
6. *Ibid.*, p. 28.
7. *Scotchman's Return*, p. 266.
8. *Two Solitudes*, p. 115.
9. *Ibid.*, pp. 27-28.
10. *Ibid.*, p. 187.
11. *Ibid.*, p. 207.

12. *Ibid.*, p. 29.
13. *Ibid.*, p. 9.
14. *Ibid.*, p. 52.
15. Woodcock, p. 134.
16. Desmond Pacey, *Creative Writing in Canada*, Toronto, The Ryerson Press, 1961, p. 219.
17. *Two Solitudes*, p. 370.
18. *Ibid.*, p. 307.
19. *Ibid.*, pp. 328-329.
20. *Ibid.*, p. 340.
21. *Ibid.*, p. 316.

Chapter IV

1. Wilson, p. 92.
2. Pacey, p. 219.
3. Woodcock, p. 135.
4. *Cross-Country*, p. 52.
5. Hugh MacLennan, *The Precipice*, Toronto, Collins, 1948, p. 8.
6. *Ibid.*, p. 96.
7. *Ibid.*, p. 132.
8. *Ibid.*, pp. 136-137.
9. *Ibid.*, p. 105.
10. *Ibid.*, pp. 157-158.
11. *Ibid.*, p. 183.

12. *Ibid.*, p. 211.
13. *Ibid.*, p. 301.
14. *Ibid.*, p. 321.
15. *Ibid.*, pp. 345-346.
16. *Ibid.*, pp. 360-361.
17. *Ibid.*, p. 370.
18. *Ibid.*, p. 67.
19. *Ibid.*, p. 71.
20. *Ibid.*, p. 305.
21. *Cross-Country*, pp. 81-82.
22. *The Precipice*, p. 23.
23. *Ibid.*, p. 129.
24. *Ibid.*, p. 161.

25. *See* John Cheever, *The Wapshot Chronicle,* New York, Harper and Row, 1954.
26. *The Precipice,* p. 169.

27. *Ibid.,* p. 26.
28. *Ibid.,* p. 217.
29. *Thirty and Three,* pp. 98-99.
30. *The Precipice,* p. 5.

Chapter V

1. R.L. MacKie, ed., *A Book of Scottish Verse,* London, Oxford University Press, The World's Classics, 1960, p. x.
2. Moray McLaren, *Understanding The Scots,* London, Frederick Muller Ltd., 1956, p. 134.
3. *Ibid.,* p. 16.
4. *Scotchman's Return,* p. 8.
5. *Ibid.,* p. 1.
6. *Ibid.*
7. Douglas Young, "For the Old Highlands," *Scottish Verse 1851-1951,* ed. Douglas Young, Edinburgh, Thomas Nelson & Sons Ltd., 1952, p. 275.
8. Wilson, pp. 100 & 103.
9. *Ibid.,* p. 65.
10. Woodcock, p. 137.
11. Hugh MacLennan, *Each Man's Son,* Toronto, MacMillan Co. of Canada Ltd., 1951, pp. viii-ix.
12. *Ibid.,* p. 26.
13. *Ibid.,* p. 27.
14. *Ibid.,* p. 40.
15. *Ibid.,* p. 60.
16. *Ibid.,* p. 63.
17. *Ibid.,* p. 63.

18. *Ibid.,* pp. 64-65.
19. *Ibid.,* p. 85.
20. *Ibid.,* p. 67.
21. *Ibid.,* p. 33.
22. *Ibid.,* p. 134.
23. *Ibid.,* p. 183.
24. *Ibid.,* pp. 189-190.
25. *Ibid.,* p. 206.
26. *Ibid.,* p. 219.
27. *Ibid.,* p. 107.
28. *Ibid.,* p. 108.
29. *Ibid.,* p. 113.
30. Ivor Brown, *Summer in Scotland,* London, Collins, 1952, p. 43.
31. *Each Man's Son,* p. 95.
32. Brown, p. 44.
33. *Each Man's Son,* p. 148.
34. *Ibid.,* p. 6.
35. *Ibid.,* p. 150.
36. *Ibid.,* p. 152.
37. *Ibid.,* pp. 167-168.
38. *Ibid.,* pp. 243-244.
39. *Scotchman's Return,* p. 276.
40. *Each Man's Son,* p. 41.
41. *Ibid.,* p. 200.
42. Woodcock, p. 137.

Chapter VI

1. Malcolm Ross, "The Watch That Ends the Night," *Queen's Quarterly,* LXVI (Summer 1959), pp. 343-344.
2. George Woodcock, *Tamarack Review,* XI (Spring 1959), p. 79.
3. Walter O'Hearn, *New York Times Book Review,* 15 February, 1959, p. 5.

4. Hugh MacLennan, "The Story of a Novel," *Masks of Fiction,* p. 37.
5. Hugh MacLennan, *The Watch That Ends the Night,* Toronto, MacMillan, 1959, pp. 3-4.
6. *Ibid.,* p. 12.
7. *Ibid.,* p. 15.
8. *Ibid.,* p. 66.
9. *Ibid.,* p. 68.

10. *Ibid.*, p. 77.
11. *Ibid.*, p. 91.
12. *Ibid.*, p. 101.
13. *Ibid.*, pp. 78-79.
14. *Ibid.*, p. 132.
15. *Ibid.*, p. 156.
16. *Ibid.*, p. 7.
17. *Ibid.*, pp. 25-26.
18. *Ibid.*, pp. 322-323.
19. *Ibid.*, p. 323.
20. *Ibid.*, p. 324.
21. *Ibid.*, p. 136.
22. *Ibid.*, pp. 154-155.
23. *Ibid.*, p. 228.
24. *Ibid.*, p. 278.
25. *Ibid.*, p. 157.
26. *Ibid.*, p. 223.
27. *Ibid.*, pp. 329-330.
28. *Ibid.*, p. 361.

29. *Ibid.*, p. 365.
30. *Ibid.*, pp. 367-368.
31. *Ibid.*, p. 317.
32. *Ibid.*, p. 113.
33. *Ibid.*, p. 114.
34. *Ibid.*, p. 204.
35. *Ibid.*, p. 129.
36. *Ibid.*, p. 17.
37. *Ibid.*, p. 142.
38. *Thirty and Three*, p. 121.
39. *The Watch That Ends the Night*, p. 355.
40. *Thirty and Three*, pp. 121-122.
41. *The Watch That Ends the Night*, pp. 353-354.
42. *Thirty and Three*, p. 122.
43. *The Watch That Ends the Night*, pp. 361-362.
44. *Ibid.*, pp. 344-345.

Chapter VII

1. Hugh MacLennan, *Return of the Sphinx*, Toronto, MacMillan of Canada, 1967, p. 160.
2. *Ibid.*, pp. 108-109.
3. *Ibid.*, p. 16.
4. *Ibid.*, p. 28.
5. *Ibid.*, pp. 43-44.
6. *Ibid.*, p. 85.
7. *Ibid.*, p. 105.
8. *Ibid.*, p. 33.

9. *Ibid.*, pp. 292-293.
10. *Ibid.*, p. 254.
11. *Ibid.*, pp. 302-303.
12. *Ibid.*, p. 267.
13. *Ibid.*, p. 182.
14. *Ibid.*, pp. 256-257.
15. *Ibid.*, pp. 39-40.
16. *Ibid.*, p. 93.
17. *Ibid.*, p. 145.
18. *Ibid.*, pp. 74-75.

Chapter VIII

1. *Scotchman's Return*, p. 157.
2. *Each Man's Son*, p. 194.
3. *The Watch That Ends the Night*, p. 17.
4. *Ibid.*, p. 195.

5. *Each Man's Son*, p. 144.
6. *Ibid.*, p. 146.
7. *The Watch That Ends the Night*, p. 323.
8. *Thirty and Three*, p. 249.

~ BIBLIOGRAPHY

PRIMARY SOURCES

Novels

MacLennan, Hugh. *Barometer Rising.* Toronto, MacMillan Co. of Canada Ltd., St. Martin's Classics, 1948.

————. *Two Solitudes.* New York, Duell, Sloan and Pearce, 1945.

————. *The Precipice.* Toronto, Collins, 1948.

————. *Each Man's Son.* Toronto, MacMillan Co. of Canada Ltd., 1951.

————. *The Watch That Ends the Night.* Toronto, MacMillan Co. of Canada Ltd., 1959.

————. *Return of the Sphinx.* Toronto, MacMillan Co. of Canada Ltd. 1967.

Volumes of Essays

MacLennan, Hugh. *Cross-Country.* Toronto, Collins, 1949.

————. *Thirty and Three,* ed., Dorothy Duncan. London, MacMillan & Co. Ltd., 1955.

————. *Scotchman's Return and other Essays.* Toronto, MacMillan Co. of Canada Ltd., 1960.

————. *Seven Rivers of Canada.* Toronto, MacMillan Co. of Canada Ltd., 1961.

Other Essays

MacLennan, Hugh. "The Story of a Novel," *Masks of Fiction,* ed. A.J.M. Smith. Canada, McClelland and Stewart Ltd., New Canadian Library, 1961, pp. 33-38.

————. "The Cabot," *MacLean's,* LXXVIII (June 5, 1965), pp. 13-14, 22 & 24.

Letters (Unpublished Material)

MacLennan, Hugh. to George Barratt, 5 March, 1935.

————. *Ibid.,* 20 October, 1941.

————. to writer, 30 July, 1965.

SECONDARY SOURCES

Books

Abrams, M.H. *A Glossary of Literary Terms.* New York, Holt Rinehart and Winston, 1960.

Allan, Ted and Gordon, Sydney. *The Scalpel, The Sword.* Boston, Little, Brown and Company, 1952.

Brown, Ivor. *Summer in Scotland.* London, Collins, 1952.

Grimble, Ian. *The Trial of Patrick Sellar.* London, Routledge and Kegan Paul, 1962.

Mackie, R.L. *A Short History of Scotland,* ed., Gordon Donaldson, Edinburgh, Oliver & Boyd, 1962.

————. Introduction to *A Book of Scottish Verse.* London, Oxford University Press, The World's Classics, 1960, pp. v-xix.

McLaren, Moray. *Understanding the Scots.* London, Frederick Muller Ltd., 1956.

Pacey, Desmond. *Creative Writing in Canada.* Toronto, Ryerson Press, 1961.

Woodcock, George. "A Nation's Odyssey," *Masks of Fiction,* ed. A.J.M. Smith, Canada, McClelland and Stewart Ltd., New Canadian Library, 1961.

————. *Literary History of Canada,* gen. ed. Carl F. Klinck. Toronto, University of Toronto Press, 1965.

Periodicals

New, William H. "Winter and the Night-People," *Canadian Literature,* No. 36, Spring, 1968.

Wilson, Edmund. "O Canada An American's Notes on Canadian Culture"—1, *The New Yorker,* 14 November, 1964.

Book Reviews

BAROMETER RISING

The Canadian Forum, XXI (December 1941), p. 282.
Queen's Quarterly, XLVIII (Winter 1941), p. 428.
Saturday Night, LVII (October 11, 1941), p. 20.

TWO SOLITUDES

The Canadian Forum, XXV (May 1945), p. 46.
Canadian Historical Review, XXVI (September 1945), pp. 326-328.
Dalhousie Review, XXV (October 1945), pp. 378-379.
Queen's Quarterly, LII (Winter 1945-46), pp. 494-496.
Saturday Night, LX (April 7, 1945), p. 21.

THE PRECIPICE

The Canadian Forum, **XXVIII** (November 1948), p. 190.
Saturday Night, LXIII (August 28, 1948), p. 17.
University of Toronto Quarterly, XVIII (April 1949), pp. 263 &
   266.

EACH MAN'S SON

The Canadian Forum, **XXXVIII** (September 1951), p. 140.
Saturday Night, LXVI (April 24, 1951), p. 35.
University of Toronto Quarterly, XXI (April 1952), pp. 263-264.

THE WATCH THAT ENDS THE NIGHT

The Canadian Forum, **XXXIX** (June 1959), p. 66.
Canadian Literature, 1 (Summer 1959), pp. 80-81.
Dalhousie Review, **XXXIX** (Spring 1959), pp. 115 & 117.
New York Times Book Review, February 15, 1959, pp. 4-5.
Queen's Quarterly, LXVI (Summer 1959), pp. 343-344.
Saturday Night, LXXIV (March 28, 1959), pp. 29 & 31.
Tamarack Review, XI (Spring 1959), pp. 77 & 79.
University of Toronto Quarterly, XXIX (July 1960), pp. 461-463.

RETURN OF THE SPHINX

New York Times Book Review, August 20, 1967, pp. 4-5.
Queen's Quarterly, LXXIV (Winter 1967), pp. 762-765.
Saturday Night, Vol. 82, No. 10 (October 1967), p. 49.
Tamarack Review, Vol. 45 (Autumn 1967), pp. 114-116.
University of Toronto Quarterly, XXXVII (July 1968), pp. 383-
   384.

~ ACKNOWLEDGEMENTS

The author gratefully acknowledges the permission to reprint excerpts from *The Trial of Patrick Sellar* by Ian Grimble, London, Routledge & Kegan Paul, 1962; from *Scotchman's Return and Other Essays* by Hugh MacLennan, Toronto, MacMillan Co. of Canada Ltd., 1960; from *Cross Country* by Hugh MacLennan, Toronto, Collins, 1949, by permission of the author; from *Thirty and Three* by Hugh MacLennan, ed. Dorothy Duncan, London, MacMillan & Co. Ltd., 1955; from "A Nation's Odyssey: The Novels of Hugh MacLennan," by George Woodcock, contained in *Masks of Fiction*, ed. A.J.M. Smith, Toronto, McClelland and Stewart Limited, New Canadian Library, 1961; from *Barometer Rising* by Hugh MacLennan, Toronto, MacMillan Co. of Canada Ltd., St. Martin's Classics, 1948; from *O Canada* by Edmond Wilson, New York, Farrar, Straus, & Giroux, 1965; from *Two Solitudes* by Hugh MacLennan, New York, Duell, Sloan & Pearce, 1945, by permission of the Meredith Corporation; from *Creative Writing in Canada*, Toronto, The Ryerson Press, 1961; from *The Precipice* by Hugh MacLennan, Toronto, Collins, 1948, by permission of the author; from *A Book of Scottish Verse*, R.L. Mackie, ed., London, Oxford University Press, The World's Classics, 1960; from *Understanding the Scots*, by Moray McLaren, London, Frederick Muller Ltd., 1956; from "For the Old Highlands," *Scottish Verse 1851-1951*, ed. Douglas Young, Edinburgh, Thomas Nelson & Sons Ltd., 1952; from *Each Man's Son* by Hugh MacLennan, Toronto, MacMillan Co. of Canada Ltd., 1951; from *Summer in Scotland* by Ivor Brown, London, Collins, 1952; from *The Watch that Ends the Night* by Hugh MacLennan, Toronto, MacMillan, 1959; from *Return of the Sphinx* by Hugh MacLennan, Toronto, MacMillan of Canada, 1967.

*Printed and bound in Canada
by Electra Printing, Montreal*

 2

990